MARX'S BASIC ONTOLOGICAL PRINCIPLES

MARX'S BASIC ONTOLOGICAL PRINCIPLES

Georg Lukács

Translated by David Fernbach

MERLIN PRESS
LONDON

Printed in Great Britain by
Whitstable Litho Ltd., Whitstable, Kent

TRANSLATOR'S NOTE

This text forms the fourth chapter of Part One of Lukács'
work *Toward the Ontology of Social Being*. It is based partly
on a manuscript that, though incomplete, was corrected by
the author, and partly on Lukács' dictated transcript.
Numbered footnotes are Lukács' own, although Lukács'
references to German-language works have generally been
replaced by references to the standard English translations.
Additional footnotes indicated by an asterisk are those
inserted by the German editors. A contents list for the
Ontology as a whole can be found at the end of this volume.

CONTENTS

> *'Categories are forms of being, characteristics of existence.'*
> Marx.

1. *Methodoligical Preliminaries*

The attempt to summarize Marx's ontology, in a theoretical sense, leads one into a somewhat paradoxical situation. On the one hand, it must be clear to any unbiassed reader of Marx that all of his concrete statements, understood correctly and without the fashionable prejudices, are in the last instance intended as direct statements about an existent, i.e. they are specifically ontological. On the other hand, however, we find in ·Marx no independent treatment of ontological problems. Marx never undertook a systematic or systematizing definition as to their specific place in thought, their distinctness from epistemology, logic, etc. This situation, with its two interconnected aspects, is undoubtedly related to Marx's decisive starting-point in Hegelian philosophy, even if this was from the beginning a critical one. As we have already seen,* there is in Hegel· a definite unity between ontology, logic and epistemology, which is a consequence of the systemic nature of his philosophy. Hegel's concept of dialectic, by its very nature, immediately unifies these three fields, and in such a way as to lead to their actual merging into one another. Thus it is only natural that the young Marx, in his earliest writings that were still governed by Hegel, was unable to formulate directly and consciously any ontological position. This negative tendency was probably strengthened by an ambiguity of Hegel's objective idealism that was only brought to light much later, particularly by Engels and Lenin. In particular,

1

while both Marx and Engels, in consciously separating themselves from Hegel, concentrated their attention, and quite
rightly, on the glaring and exclusive opposition between
Hegel's idealism and their own new materialism, both
polemically and in their actual presentation, they later came
to stress energetically the effectively materialist tendencies
that were already latent in objective idealism. Thus Engels
writes in his *Ludwig Feuerbach* of Hegel's 'materialism
[idealistically] turned upside down',[1] and Lenin of the
approaches to materialism in Hegel's *Logic*.[2] It must also be
stressed, of course, that Marx himself, even in his sharpest
polemics against left Hegelians such as Bruno Bauer and Max
Stirner, never identified their idealism with that of Hegel.

The turning-point that Feuerbach represented in the process
of the dissolution of Hegelian philosophy had undoubtedly
an ontological character, since it was Feuerbach who, for the
first time in German development, opposed idealism and
materialism openly, on a broad front, and with penetrating
effect. Even the weaknesses in his position that later came to
light, e.g. his confinement to the abstract relationship
between god and man, contributed towards bringing the
question of ontology abruptly and distinctly to consciousness.
This effect is most transparent in the case of the young
Engels, who, from his beginnings in the 'Young Germany'
movement that had little philosophical clarity, developed
into a left Hegelian; here we can see how radical was the first
effect of the new ontological orientation derived from
Feuerbach. The fact that nothing came out of this in the
long run except a pale new version of the materialism of the
18th century, with the exception of Gottfried Keller and the
Russian revolutionary democrats, in no way alters the
intensity of this new departure. Yet there is little sign of such
a convulsion in Marx. His writings show rather an acknowledgement of Feuerbach that is positive and understanding, but
that always remains critical and demands further critical

2

development. This is visible in early letters (already in 1841), and then later, in the midst of the struggle against the Hegelians' idealism, it is formulated quite unambiguously, in the *German Ideology:* 'As far as Feuerbach is a materialist he does not deal with history, and as far as he considers history he is not a materialist.'[3] Marx's judgement of Feuerbach thus always has two sides to it: acknowledgement of his ontological turn as the only serious philosophical act of that period, and at the same time the establishment of his limits, i.e. that Feuerbach's German materialism completely ignored the problem of the ontology of social being. This does not simply demonstrate Marx's philosophical clarity and universality; it is a position that also throws light on his own earlier development, on the central place that the ontological problems of social being assumed in it.

A glance at Marx's doctoral dissertation is instructive in this regard. In this context, Marx comes to speak of Kant's logical and epistemological criticism of the ontological proof for the existence of god, and objects: 'The proofs of the existence of God are either mere *hollow tautologies.* Take for instance the ontological proof. This only means: "that which I conceive for myself in a real way *(realiter),* is a real concept for me", something that works on me. In this sense *all gods,* the pagan as well as the Christian ones, have possessed a real existence. Did not the ancient Moloch reign? Was not the Delphic Apollo a real power in the life of the Greeks? Kant's critique means nothing in this respect. If somebody imagines that he has a hundred talers, if this concept is not for him an arbitrary, subjective one, if he believes in it, then these hundred imagined talers have for him the same value as a hundred real ones. For instance, he will incur debts on the strength of his imagination, his imagination will *work, in the way as all humanity has incurred debts on its gods.'*[4]

We can already trace here some of the most important elements of Marx's thought. Paramount here is the fact that social reality is seen as the ultimate criterion for the social existence or non-existence of a phenomenon, which certainly reveals a broad and deep problematic which the young Marx was not yet able at that time to master ontologically. For the general spirit of his dissertation leads on the one hand to the conclusion that he did not allow the existence of any kind of god; while on the other hand the actual historical efficacy of certain ideas of god should lead to these having a kind of social existence. Thus Marx already raises here a problem that was later to play an important role for a Marx who had already become an economist and materialist: i.e. the practical social function of certain forms of consciousness, irrespective of whether they are true or false in a general ontological sense. These ideas that are important for the later development of Marx's thought are developed in an interesting way in this criticism of Kant. Kant attacked the so-called ontological proof on the basis of logic and epistemology, in so far as he rejected any necessary connection between idea and reality, and completely denied that the content had any ontologically relevant character. The young Marx protests against this—again in the name of the ontological specificity of social existence—and ingeniously points out how in certain circumstances a hundred imaginary talers could very well acquire a relevant social existence. (In Marx's later economics, this dialectic between ideal and real money appears as an important element in the relationship between money as a means of circulation and its function as a means of payment.)

We have already seen in considering Hegel how Marx, in the name of the concrete ontological specificity of social forms, called for their concrete ontological investigation, and rejected Hegel's method of presenting relationships of this kind on the basis of logical schemas. This clearly shows, in the course of development of the young Marx, a tendency towards the increasing concretization of forms and relationships, etc.

4

of social existence, which reached a philosophical turning-point precisely in his economic studies. These tendencies find their first adequate expression in the *Economic and Philosophical Manuscripts,* since it is not the least aspect of the path-breaking originality of these texts that for the first time in the history of philosophy the categories of economics appear as those of the production and reproduction of human life, and hence make it possible to depict social existence ontologically on a materialist basis. Yet the economic centre of Marx's ontology in no way means that his view of the world is 'economist'. (This conception first emerges in Marx's epigones, who had lost all inkling of Marx's philosophical method, and it contributed very much towards distorting and compromising Marxism philosophically.) Marx's philosophical development towards materialism culminated in this turn towards economics; it is impossible to establish beyond doubt whether and how far Feuerbach played a significant role in this, although Marx agreed immediately, in principle, with Feuerbach's ontological and anti-religious views inspired by natural philosophy. It is just as certain, however, that in this area, too, Marx was very quick to criticize and go beyond Feuerbach: in natural philosophy, he always took up a clear position against the traditional separation of nature and society that Feuerbach had not overcome, and always considered the problem of nature predominantly from the standpoint of its interaction with society. Thus the opposition to Hegel is still sharper in Marx than in Feuerbach himself. Marx only recognizes a single science, that of history, which deals with nature as well as with the world of men.[5] In the question of religion, he was not satisfied with the abstract and contemplative relationship between man and god, and counter-posed to Feuerbach's crude, if materialistically inspired, ontology, the demand for a concrete and materialist treatment of all relations of human life, in particular those of society and its history. This throws a completely new ontological light on the problem of nature.

Since Marx made the production and reproduction of human life into the central question, man himself, as well as all his objects, conditions, relationships, etc. acquires the double determination of an insuperable natural basis and the permanent social transformation of this. As in all Marx's work, labour is here too the central category, in which all other determinations already manifest themselves *in nuce:* 'So far therefore as labour is a creator of use-value, is useful labour, it is a necessary condition, independent of all forms of society, for the existence of the human race; it is an eternal nature-imposed necessity, without which there can be no material exchanges between man and Nature, and therefore no life.'[6] Labour gives rise to a double transformation. On the one hand the working man himself is transformed by his labour; by working on external nature he also changes his own, 'develops his slumbering powers and compels them to act in obedience to his sway'. On the other hand, natural objects and natural forces are transformed into means and objects of labour, raw materials, etc. The worker 'makes use of the mechanical, physical, and chemical properties of some substances in order to make other substances subservient to his aims.' Here natural objects remain what they naturally were, in so far as their properties, relationships, conditions, etc. exist independent of human consciousness and can only be made useful by a correct recognition of these which is set in motion by labour. This 'making useful', however, is a teleological process. 'At the end of every labour-process, we get a result that already existed in the imagination of the labourer at its commencement. He not only effects a change of form in the material on which he works, but he also realises a purpose of his own that gives the law to his *modus operandi,* and to which he must subordinate his will.'[7] We shall deal with the ontological significance of teleology in labour in a special chapter in the second part of this work.*

For the present we shall confine ourselves to characterizing the starting-point of Marx's ontology of social being in its most general features.

The following elements should be particularly stressed. Above all, social being presupposes in general and in all specific processes the existence of inorganic and organic nature. Social being cannot be conceived as independent from natural being and as its exclusive opposite, as a great number of bourgeois philosophers do with respect to the so-called 'spiritual sphere'. Marx's ontology of social being just as sharply rules out a simple, vulgar materialist transfer of natural laws to society, as was fashionable for example in the era of 'social Darwinism'. The objective forms of social being grow out of natural being in the course of the rise and development of social practice, and become ever more expressly social. This growth is certainly a dialectical process, which begins with a leap, with the teleological project *(Setzung)* in labour, for which there is no analogy in nature. This ontological leap is in no way negated by the fact that it involves in reality a very lengthy process, with innumerable transitional forms. With the act of teleological projection *(Setzung)* in labour, social being itself is now there. The historical process of its development involves the most important transformation of this 'in itself' into a 'for itself', and hence the tendency towards the overcoming of merely natural forms and contents of being by forms and contents that are ever more pure and specifically social.

The teleological project *(Setzung)* as a form of material transformation of material reality remains something fundamentally new from the ontological point of view. Genetically, of course, its existence has to be explained via its transitional forms. Yet these can only themselves be given a correct ontological interpretation if their result, labour in the true sense of the word, is correctly understood in its ontological significance, and if the attempt is made to understand this genetic process, which in itself is in no way teleological, in terms of its result. This is not just the case with this fundamental relationship. Marx consistently stressed this mode of conceiving things as a general method in society:

'Bourgeois society is the most developed and the most complex historic organization of production. The categories which express its relations, the comprehension of its structure, thereby also allow insights into the structure and the relations of production of all the vanished social formations out of whose ruins and elements it built itself up, whose partly still unconquered remnants are carried along within it, whose mere nuances have developed explicit significance within it, etc. Human anatomy contains a key to the anatomy of the ape. The intimations of higher development among the subordinate animal species, however, can be understood only after the higher development is already known. The bourgeois economy thus supplies the key to the ancient, etc.'[8]

Just after this passage, Marx protests against any attempt at 'modernization', i.e. the transfer of categories from a more developed stage to a more primitive one. But this is simply a defence against obvious and often present misunderstandings. The essential thing in this methodological position still remains the precise separation of the real, as a process that exists in itself, from the ways by which it comes to be known. As we shall see in more detail in Marx's criticism, Hegel's idealist illusion arises precisely from his failure to make a sufficient distinction between the ontological process of being and development and the epistemologically necessary process of comprehension, in fact from seeing the latter as a substitute for the former, and even an ontologically higher form of it.

If we return from this necessary excursus to the ontological relationship between nature and society, then we find that the categories and laws of nature, organic as well as inorganic, provide a basis for social categories that is in the last analysis (in the sense of a fundamental alteration of their essence) irreducible. Only on the basis of at least an immediate knowledge of the real properties of things and processes is it possible for the teleological project *(Setzung)* of labour to fulfil its transformative function. The fact that completely new forms of objectivity now arise, which have no analogy in nature, in no way alters this state of affairs. Even if the natural object seems to remain directly nature-like, its function as a use-value is already something qualitatively new in relation to nature, and with the objective social formation of use-value there arises in the course of social development exchange-value, in which, if it is considered in isolation, any nature-like objectivity vanishes; as Marx puts it, it consists of an 'unsubstantial reality'.[9] At one point Marx remarks ironically against certain economists, 'So far no chemist has ever discovered exchange-value either in a pearl or a diamond.'[10] On the other hand, however, a purely social objectivity of this kind, even if it is highly mediated, still presupposes socially transformed natural objectivities (no exchange-value without use-value, etc.), so that while there are certainly purely social categories, and indeed their ensemble is what composes the specificity of social being, this being does not simply rise above natural being in the concrete material process of its genesis, but constantly reproduces itself in this framework, and can never separate itself completely (in the ontological sense) from this basis. The expression 'never completely' must be stressed here, for the essential tendency in the self-formation of social being consists precisely in that purely natural determinations are replaced by ontological mixtures of natural-ness and sociality (we need only think of domestic animals), and the purely social determinations develop further on this foundation. The main tendency of the developmental process that arises in this way is the constant increase, both quantitative and qualitative, of purely or predominantly social components, the 'retreat of the natural boundary', as Marx puts it. Without going further into this complex of problems at this point, it is already possible to say that the materialist turning-point in the ontology of social being, which was brought about by the discovery of the ontological priority of the economy within it, presupposes a materialist ontology of nature.

This indissoluble unity of materialism in Marx's ontology is not a function of the degree to which Marxist scholars have managed to depict these relationships concretely and convincingly in the various fields of natural science. Marx himself spoke of the single science of history long before tendencies of this kind had been discovered in the real world. It is certainly not by chance that Marx and Engels, for all their reservations, greeted the appearance of Darwin's work as a 'foundation for our opinion',[11] that Engels enthusiastically supported the Kant-Laplace hypothesis in astronomy, etc. The importance of a further and contemporary development of Marxism in this sense can not be overestimated. Here it must simply be stressed that the foundation of a materialist ontology of nature, which brings together historicity, the form of process, dialectical contradiction, etc., is implicitly contained in the methodological foundation of Marx's ontology.

At this point it seems appropriate to outline in a few words the new type that Marx's conception represents in the history of philosophy and science. Marx never put forward an express claim to have created a specific philosophical method, let alone a philosophical system. In the 1840s, Marx struggled in philosophy against the idealism of Hegel, and particularly against the idealism of Hegel's radical pupils, which was becoming ever more subjective. After the interruption of the 1848 revolution, the foundation of a science of economics came to form the focal point of his work. Many who esteem his early philosophical writings of the 1840s draw the conclusion from this that Marx turned away from philosophy and became 'simply' an economic specialist. This is a very hasty conclusion, which closer consideration shows to be completely untenable. It is based purely on external criteria, on the dominant methodology of the second half of the 19th century, which decreed a mechanically rigid opposition between philosophy and the various positive sciences, and hence degraded philosophy itself, by way of its exclusive foundation in logic and epistemology, to a specific science. From a standpoint of this kind, bourgeois science and the modes of thought influenced by it, even among supporters of Marxism, came to see the economics of the mature Marx as a specific science, in contrast to the philosophical tendencies of his youth. And at a later date there were many who, particularly under the influence of existentialist subjectivism, constructed an opposition between the two periods of Marx's work.

Our later and more detailed discussion will clearly demonstrate the feebleness of a contrast of this kind between the young, philosophical, Marx and the later pure economist with no specific standpoint. We shall see that Marx in no way became 'less philosophical', but on the contrary significantly deepened his philosophical conceptions in all fields. We need only refer to the supersession of the Hegelian dialectic, something that is purely philosophical. Even in Marx's youth we can find significant approaches to this, particularly where he sought to escape from a doctrine of contradiction which had been erected into a logical absolute.[12] The over-hasty critics of the philosopher Marx particularly overlook, among other things, those passages in *Capital* where Marx, precisely while basing himself in economics, formulates a quite new conception of the abolition of contradictions:

'We saw in a former chapter that the exchange of commodities implies contradictory and mutually exclsuive conditions. The differentiation of commodities into commodities and money does not sweep away these inconsistencies, but develops a *modus vivendi*, a form in which they can exist side by side. This is generally the way in which real contradictions are reconciled. For instance, it is a contradiction to depict one body as constantly falling towards another, and as, at the same time, constantly flying away from it. The ellipse is a form of motion which, while allowing this contradiction to go on, at the same time reconciles it.'[13]

This conception of contradiction, which is purely ontological, shows contradiction to be the permanent motor of the dynamic inter-relation of complexes and of the processes that arise from relations of this kind. Contradiction is thus not only, as with Hegel, the form of sudden transition from one stage to another, but rather the driving force of a normal process. Certainly, the sudden transition with its crisis-like character as a qualitative leap is in no way rejected. But knowledge of these leaps now depends on the discovery of the specific conditions under which they appear; they are no longer purely 'logical' consequences of an abstract contradiction. As Marx shows here with great clarity, this can also be the vehicle of a normally occurring process; contradiction shows itself to be a principle of being precisely in so far as it can be found in reality as the basis of processes of this kind.

Serious consideration allows us to confidently brush aside the kind of error referred to above. The economic works of the mature Marx are certainly consistently centred on the scientificity of economics, but they have nothing in common with the bourgeois conception of economics as simply one specific science: this conception isolates so-called phenomena of pure economics from the total inter-relations of social being as a whole, and analyses these in an artificial way that—in principle—allows the area thus elaborated to be put in an abstract connection with another that is just as artificially isolated (law, sociology, etc.), whereas Marx's economics always starts from the totality of social being and always flows back again into it. As we have already explained, the central and (occasionally) often immanent treatment of economic phenomena has its basis in the fact that the decisive driving force of the overall social development, in the last analysis, is to be sought and found here. All that this economics has in common with the contemporary and later specific science of the same name is the negative feature that they both reject the *a priori* constructive method of earlier philosophers (including Hegel) and see the real foundation for science as consisting only in the facts themselves and their connections. Yet if they have this in common, it does not make them the same. It is certainly possible to describe every procedure that starts from the facts and rejects abstractly constructed relationships as empirical, but this expression, even in the customary sense, can encompass extremely heterogenous orientations to the facts. The old empiricism often had a very naive ontological character: it took as its starting-point the irreducible existence of these given facts, naively remained essentially at the level of direct data of this kind, and left out of account the further mediations, which were frequently the decisive ontological relationships. In the later empiricism that came into existence on the basis of a positivist or even neopositivist foundation, this naive, uncritical ontology disappeared, but only to be replaced by abstractly constructed categories of manipulation. Significant natural scientists developed the spontaneous ontological position into what various idealist philosophers have labelled 'naive realism'; but with scientists such as Boltzmann or Planck it is scarcely any longer naive, and distinguishes very precisely the real concrete character of definite phenomena and groups of phenomena within the concrete field of research. What is still lacking, however, for the naïveté to be overcome, is 'simply' the philosophical awareness of what is actually done by these scientists in their own practice, so that complexes that are recognized correctly in the scientific sense are sometimes artificially coupled together with a world outlook that is of a completely different nature. In the social sciences there are few examples of a 'naive realism'; the claim to have confined oneself to the facts generally leads to superficial re-editions of empiricism, while pragmatic adherence to the immediately given facticity excludes important and actually existing relationships which are less directly apparent from the overall conception, and thus often leads objectively to a falsification of the fetishized and deified facts.

It is only by demarcating it in this way on all sides that it is possible to adequately present the ontological character of Marx's economic writings. These are specifically works of science, and in no way works of philosophy. But their scientific character is reached through philosophy, and never leaves it behind, so that every establishment of a fact, every acknowledgment of a relationship, is not simply critically elaborated from the direct factual correctness, but rather, proceeding from this and equally continually going beyond it, all facticity is investigated from the standpoint of its real existential content, its ontological nature. Science grows out of life, and in life itself, whether we realize this or not, we have spontaneously to behave ontologically. The transition to science can make this tendency, which is itself unavoidable, more conscious and critical, but it can also weaken it, or even make it vanish. Marx's economics is permeated by a scientific spirit which never abandons this process of making conscious and critical, in the ontological sense, but rather applies it, as a constantly effective critical measure, in every process of establishing a fact or relationship. To speak quite generally, what is involved here is thus a scientificity which never loses its connection with the spontaneous ontological orientation of everyday life, but on the contrary continuously purifies this critically and develops it to a higher level; and which consciously elaborates the ontological determinations that necessarily lie at the basis of every science. It is precisely here that it clearly sets itself in opposition to any kind of constructive philosophy, whether logical or otherwise. But a critical defence against the false ontologies that arise in philosophy in no way means that this scientificity takes up an ultimately anti-philosophical position. On the contrary. What is involved is rather a consciously critical collaboration between the spontaneous ontology of everyday life and scientific and philosophical correctness. Marx's turn against the abstract constructions of idealist philosophy which violate reality is a special case of this. A critical perspective, critical rejection of contemporary science, can in certain circumstances be a major task in this connection. As Engels wrote, correctly, on the situation in the 17th and 18th centuries: 'It is to the highest credit of the philosophy of the time that it did not let itself be led astray by the restricted state of contemporary natural knowledge, and that—from Spinoza down to the great French materialists—it insisted on explaining the world from the world itself and left the justification in detail to the natural sciences of the future.'[14] A criticism of the same kind, naturally with a completely different content, is also a necessary task in the present situation: the purging from science of neopositivist prejudices, which are no longer just confined principally to the area of philosophy in the narrow sense, but also essentially deform the sciences themselves.

It is not the place here to deal with these problems in detail. We simply want to make clear Marx's method on what is clearly a question of key importance. It is precisely with problems of social being that the ontological problem of difference, opposition, and the relationship of appearance and essence, plays a decisive role. Even in everyday life, phenomena often conceal the essence of their own being, instead of illuminating it. In favourable historical conditions, science can accomplish a great task of purification here, as it did for instance in the Renaissance and in the Enlightenment. But historical conjunctures can also arise in which the process occurs in the opposite direction: correct approaches or even mere suspicions of everyday life are obscured by science, and are turned round in an incorrect sense. (Nikolai Hartmann's fruitful intuition of the *'intentio recta',* as we have shown earlier, suffers particularly from the fact that he does not take account of this highly important process as a whole.) Hobbes already saw clearly that attitudes of this kind were more frequent and stronger in the area of social being than in that of nature; he also indicated the cause of this, i.e. the role of action governed by interest.[15] There can of course also be an interest of this kind in questions of nature, particularly in relation to their implications for general world outlook; it is sufficient to recall here the debates over Copernicus or Darwin. But since action governed by interest forms an essential ontological component of social being that cannot be eliminated, the biassing effect of this on the facts and their ontological character acquires here a qualitatively significant new importance; quite irrespective of the fact that these ontological attitudes do not affect the intrinsic being of nature itself, while in social being they can become, as attitudes, dynamically effective elements of the intrinsically existing totality.

Marx's assertion that 'all science would be superfluous if the outward appearance and the essence of things directly coincided',[16] is thus extremely important for the ontology of social being. In and for itself, this thesis has a general ontological value, and applies to nature as well as to society. It will later be shown, however, that the relation between appearance and essence in social being displays new features and determinations, as a result of its inseparable connection with practice. To bring up just one example here, it is an important part of this relationship that in every (relatively) completed process, the genesis of the finished product directly disappears in the result. Scientific presentations very often develop in such a way that the direct and apparently already completed character of the product is recalled in thought, and its character as a process, which is not directly perceivable, is no longer made visible. (Whole sciences, such as geology, for example, have arisen on the basis of presentations of this kind.) In the region of social being, however, the process of emergence is a teleological one. This has the result that its product only assumes the phenomenal form of something ready and complete, in which its own genesis directly vanishes, if the outcome corresponds to the goal aimed at; otherwise its incompleteness precisely refers back to the process of its emergence. I have deliberately chosen an extremely simplified example. The particular character of the relation of appearance and essence in social being also involves action governed by interest, and if this involves the interests of social groups, as is generally the case, then science can easily slip out of its controlling role and become an instrument which serves to conceal the essence and make it vanish, precisely in the sense that Hobbes already recognized. It is therefore not by chance that Marx put forward this thesis on the nature of science and the relation of appearance and essence in the context of a criticism of the vulgar economists: in the course of a polemic against forms of appearance that were conceived and interpreted in a manner that was absurd from the ontological point of view, and that completely suppressed the real relationships. Marx's philosophical assertion thus has here the function of an ontological criticism of false ideas, a call for scientific awareness by means of the re-establishment in thought of the genuine reality as this exists in itself. This kind of presentation is typical of the internal construction of the work of the mature Marx. It is a construction of a completely new character: a scientificity which, in its process of generalization, never loses this level, but always keeps in view, in every single fact it establishes, and in every concrete relationship it reconstructs in thought, the totality of social being, and considers the reality and the significance of an individual phenomenon from this standpoint; an ontological and philosophical treatment of the reality as this exists in itself, which never soars above the phenomenon under consideration with an autonomization of abstractions, but rather struggles to attain the highest stage of awareness of it, by criticism and self-criticism, precisely in order to be able to concretely comprehend every existent in the form of being that is precisely specific to it. We believe that Marx created in this way a new form of general scientificity as well as a new ontology, and one which is destined in the future to overcome the deeply problematic character of modern scientificity, which persists despite the wealth of newly discovered facts. In their criticisms of Hegel, the classics of Marxism always stressed the struggle against his system. This was quite correct, for it was precisely here that were centred all those philosophical tendencies that Marx most decisively disavowed. With its ideal of philosophical synthesis, the system involves in particular the principle of completion and closure, ideas that are completely incompatible with the ontological historicity of an existent, and already led to irresolvable antinomies in Hegel's own work. A static ideal unity of this kind, however, arises inevitably once categories are ordered in a specific hierarchical relationship. The very attempt to produce a hierarchical arrangement of this kind contradicts Marx's ontological conception. Not that the idea of the super- and sub-ordination of forms was something foreign to him; we already indicated in our presentation of Hegel that it was precisely Marx who introduced the idea of the predominant moment in his treatment of reciprocal action.

However a hierarchic system is not only something that exists for all time, it also has to render its categories homogenous, in order to arrange them in a definitive connection (even at the cost of impoverishing or violating their content), and reduce them as far as possible to a single dimension of their relationship. Those thinkers who have had a genuine ontological sense for the rich and varied character of the dynamic structure of reality have precisely come to focus their interest on those kinds of relationship which cannot be adequately brought into any kind of system. It is just here that this opposition to systematization has a character precisely opposed to that of an equally anti-systematic empiricism. We already recognized in the latter, here and there, a naive ontologism, i.e. a regard for the reality of direct appearances, for individual things and easily perceivable surface relationships. But because this orientation to reality is one that, even if genuine, is merely peripheral, the empiricist, if he ventures only a little beyond the field with which he is spontaneously familiar, can easily get entangled in the most fantastic intellectual adventures.[17] The criticism of systems that we accept, and that we find consciously developed in Marx, proceeds on the contrary from the totality of the existent, and seeks to comprehend this as closely as possible in all its intricate and manifold relationships. Here the totality is in no way formal and simply ideal, but rather the reproduction in thought of the really existing, and the categories are not building blocks of a hierarchical system, but actually are 'forms of being, characteristics of existence', elements for the construction of relatively total, real and dynamic complexes, whose reciprocal inter-relations produce ever more comprehensive complexes, both in an extensive and in an intensive sense. In the face of adequate knowledge of these complexes, logic loses its leading role in philosophy; it becomes one special science alongside any other, as the means to comprehend the laws governing pure and hence homogenous patterns of thought. The role of philosophy, however, is only negated in the dual Hegelian sense: it remains the guiding principle of this new scientificity, as an ontological criticism of being of all kind, if without the claim to dominate and subordinate phenomena and their relationships. It is thus not by chance, nor simply a product of the contingencies of the history of science, that the mature Marx entitled his economic works not Economics, but the 'Critique of Political Economy'. This does of course directly refer to the criticism of the ideas of the bourgeois economists, which was itself very important; but it also involves, in its stress on the permanent and immanent ontological criticism of facticity of any kind, a criticism of any relation, of any law-like connection.

Certainly this new development did not suddenly spring like Pallas Athene from the head of Zeus. It was necessarily the product of a long and uneven development. In the negative sense, the—often spontaneous—criticism of philosophical principles that subject reality to hierarchical violation, leads to attempts of this kind. As consciously and clearly expressed in Marx himself, this criticism, levelled at the most thought out and formally most complete system, that of Hegel, led to the elaboration of the new style of thought. There had also been beginnings in the positive sense, however, where conscious recognition of the primary existence of major complexes of being began to develop, where, in connection with the criticism of idealist systemic thought, the new kind, which is needed to comprehend complexes of this kind, began to dawn. I believe that certain of Aristotles' texts, particularly the *Nicomachean Ethics,* already represent an experiment in this direction, with the criticism of Plato playing the negative role here referred to. The first great scientific attempt in the Renaissance to comprehend social being in an all-round way as being, and to eliminate these system-principles that inhibit the knowledge of being, in other words Machiavelli's attempt, also belongs here,[18] as does Vico's search to comprehend the historicity of the social world ontologically. But it was only in Marx's ontology that these tendencies received a philosophically mature and fully conscious form.

Even though this overall conception arose from the materialist criticism and superseding of Hegel's method, it was foreign to the dominant tendencies of the time and could thus not be understood as a method either by its opponents or by its supporters. After 1848, the collapse of Hegelian philosophy, and particularly after the victory of neo-Kantianism and positivism, this understanding of ontological problems disappeared. The neo-Kantians even ejected from philosophy the unknowable thing-in-itself, and as far as positivism was concerned, the subjective perception of the world simply coincided with its reality. It was no wonder, then, that for a public opinion among scientists that was influenced in this way, Marxian economics was seen simply as a particular individual science, which however inevitably appeared inferior, from the standpoint of bourgeois methodology, in its application of the 'precise' scientific division of labour and the 'value-free' mode of presentation. It was not long after Marx's death that even the overwhelming majority of his declared supporters in philosophy found themsleves under the influence of tendencies of this kind. In so far as there was a Marxist orthodoxy, its content consisted essentially in individual and often misunderstood assertions and conclusions of Marx's that were erected into radical slogans; this was, for example, how the supposed law of absolute immiseration developed, with the help of Kautsky. It was to no avail that Engels, particularly in the form of criticism and advice in his letters, sought to loosen this rigidity and bring it back to a genuine dialectic. It is very characteristic that these letters were first published by Bernstein in the belief that they would strengthen the revisionist tendencies among Marxists. The fact that the dialectical flexibility demanded by Engels, the abandonment of rigidified vulgarization, could be conceived in such a way, shows that the two competing tendencies equally failed to understand the methodological essence of Marx's doctrine. Even Marxist theorists who made important contributions to many particular questions, such as Rosa Luxemburg and Franz Mehring, had little feeling for the basic philosophical tendencies in the work of Marx. While Bernstein, Max Adler and many others hoped to find a 'supplement' to Marxism in Kant's philosophy, and Friedrich Adler and others sought this 'supplement' in Mach, the politically radical Mehring denied that Marxism had anything at all to do with philosophy.

It was only Lenin who set under way a real Marx Renaissance. The *Philosophical Notebooks* that he wrote during the early years of the War, in particular, go back once again to the really central problems of Marx's thought; the detailed and continually deepening critical understanding of the Hegelian dialectic culminates in a sharp renunciation of the former Marxism: 'It is impossible completely to understand Marx's *Capital,* and especially its first chapter, without having thoroughly studied and understood the *whole* of Hegel's *Logic.* Consequently, half a century later none of the Marxists understood Marx!!'[19] Nor does Lenin make an exception of Plekhanov, whom he otherwise valued theoretically, and who was more familiar with Hegel than anyone else among the Marxists of that time.[20] He successfully follows here the course set by the late Engels, deepening and continuing his work in many questions. It should not remain unmentioned, of course, that Engels, as we shall see in connection with some important particular questions, was less consistent and deep than Marx himself, and took over unaltered from Hegel—even if with a materialist reversal—much that Marx rejected on the basis of deeper ontological consideration, or at least decisively modified. The distinction between the completely independent way that the young Marx overcame the fundamentals of the entire Hegelian philosophy, and the way that Engels overcame his philosophical idealism under the influence of Feuerbach, also shows definite effects in their later writings. Lenin can of course not just be

characterized as a continuer of Engels, but there are nevertheless certain questions that allow such a relationship to be
established. Yet it should equally be noted that it is
occasionally hard to decide how far this is a question of mere
terminology and how far real problems are involved. Thus
Lenin says of the relation of *Capital* to a general dialectical
philosophy: 'If Marx did not leave behind him a *'Logic'*...,
he did leave the *logic* of *Capital*. ... In *Capital*, Marx
applied to a single science logic, dialectics and the theory of
knowledge of materialism (three words are not needed: it is
one and the same thing) which has taken everything valuable
in Hegel and developed it further.'[21]

It is Lenin's great merit, and not simply in this instance,
that he was the only Marxist of his time who decisively
rejected the modern philosophical supremacy of autonomously
founded (and necessarily idealist) logic and epistemology,
and referred back, as here, to the original Hegelian conception
of the unity of logic, epistemology and dialectics, of course
in a materialist sense. It should further be noted that,
particularly in *Materialism and Empirio-Criticism*, Lenin's
epistemology, as the reflection of a material reality existing
outside of consciousness, is in practice always subordinated
to a materialist ontology. It is also possible here to interpret
the objective content of the dialectic assumed in this unity
ontologically.

It is certain, however, as we shall see in a moment in
analysing Marx's only discussion of a general methodological
and philosophical character, that Marx did not accept the
unity asserted here, and that he not only distinctly separated
ontology and epistemology from one another, but also saw
in the failure to maintain such a separation one of the sources
of Hegel's idealist illusions. But even if a detailed consideration of Lenin's philosophical work gives rise to certain
objections such as these in connection with his supersession
of the Hegelian dialectic and its use in the further develop-

ment of Marxism (and I believe that a critical all-round presentation of Lenin as a philosopher is one of the most important and necessary investigations today, since his ideas are used on all sides), it still remains that Lenin's work represents the single large-scale attempt since the death of Engels to re-establish Marxism in its totality, to apply it to the problems of the present and in this way develop it further. Only unfavourable historical circumstances prevented Lenin's work from having a broad and deep theoretical and methodological effect.

The great revolutionary crisis that developed out of the First World War and the rise of the Soviet republic, certainly aroused in many countries a new and fresh study of Marxism that was not distorted by the bourgeoisified traditions of social democracy.[22] However the long-term tendency was towards the suppression of Marx and Lenin by Stalin's policy, and we still lack today a critical historical presentation of this. There is no question but that Stalin at first emerged as the defender of Lenin's doctrine, particularly against Trotsky, and several publications of this time, up till the beginning of the 1930s, tended to carry on the Leninist renewal of Marxism against the ideology of the Second International. Yet however correct the stress on what was new in Lenin, it had the consequence in the Stalin period that the study of Marx was slowly pressed into the background by that of Lenin. And this development culminated, particularly after the publication of the *History of the CPSU(B)* (with its chapter on philosophy) in the suppression of Lenin by Stalin. From this time onwards, official philosophy was reduced to commentary on Stalin's publications. Marx and Lenin were only brought in in the form of supporting quotations. It is not the place here to present the devastating consequences for theory in more detail. This, too, would be a most important task today, and would often be of practical significance. (We need only think of the way that the official

24

theory of planning quite ignores Marx's theory of social reproduction.) There arose what Marxist terminology calls a complete and completely arbitrary subjectivism, which was suited to justifying any decisions whatever as necessary consequences of Marxism-Leninism. This situation can only be asserted here. But if Marxism today is again to become a living force in philosophical development, then we must go back on all questions to Marx himself; these efforts can certainly be supported in many ways by the works of Engels and Lenin, while in treatments of the kind that we have begun to embark on, the period of the Second International, as well as that of Stalin, can confidently be left unmentioned, much as the sharpest criticism of it from the standpoint of re-establishing the reputation of Marx's doctrine is an important task.

2. *The Critique of Political Economy*

The mature Marx wrote relatively little on general philosophical and scientific questions. The plan for a brief presentation of the rational kernel of Hegel's dialectic, which occasionally appears, was never realized. The only text that we have of Marx on this theme, and a fragmentary one at that, is the *Introduction* that he wrote in the late 1850s when he sought to give a finished form to his economic work. This fragment was published by Kautsky in the 1907 edition of the book that came out of Marx's work at that time, *A Contribution to the Critique of Political Economy*. More than half a century has passed since then, and yet we cannot say that this text has ever really influenced conceptions of the nature and method of Marx's doctrine. This sketch, however, summarizes the most essential problems of the ontology of social being, and the consequent methods to be employed by economic research as the central area of this level of material existence. Its neglect is the result of a factor that we have already mentioned, and that is generally not consciously realized: abandonment of the critique of political economy and its replacement by simple economics as a science in the bourgeois sense.

Right at the beginning, we have to stress the methodological point that Marx consistently and sharply separated two complexes: social being, which exists independent of whether it is more or less correctly understood, and the method most suitable to comprehend it in thought. Thus not only is the priority of the ontological over mere knowledge related to being in general, but the entire objective reality with its concrete structure and dynamic, just as it is, is of the highest ontological importance. This was Marx's philosophical position as early as the *Economic and Philosophical Manuscripts.* In these studies he treated the reciprocal relations of objective reality as the original form of every ontological relation between existents:

'A being which has no object outside itself is not an objective being. A being which is not itself an object for a third being has no being for its *object,* i.e. it has no objective relationships and its existence is not objective. A non-objective being is a *non-being.*'[1]

Here already Marx rejects any idea that certain 'ultimate' elements of being have an ontological priority over the more complex and compound ones, or that the synthetic functions of the knowing subject play a role of some kind in the nature and form of their objectivity. It was Kant who put forward in its most typical form the theory of the synthetic construction of the actual concrete objectivity, in contrast to the abstract thing-in-itself that was always beyond consciousness and hence unknowable, so that it was the knowing subject who performed the actual concrete synthesis, even if in a way prescribed to him by natural law. Since it was at first the Kantian influence, which lasted for a long while, that was mainly responsible for preventing the development of Marxist ontology, it is useful to indicate briefly this radical opposition, since despite many changes in the bourgeois world view, it has never completely lost its actuality.

If objectivity is a primary ontological property of all being, then this leads to the assertion that the existent itself is always a dynamic totality, a unity of complexity and process. Since Marx was concerned with social being, this central position of the ontological category of totality was more directly given for him than it is in the case of the philosophical investigation of nature. In the latter case, it is often possible simply to add in the category of totality, even in a vigorous way, while in society, the totality is always directly given. (This is not contradicted by the fact that Marx treats the world economy and hence world history also as the resultant of the historical process.) The young Marx already recognized and asserted quite clearly that every society forms a totality.[2] However, this is merely the most general principle, and in no way indicates the nature and properties of such a totality, let alone the way in which it is directly given and the way it is possible to arrive at an adequate knowledge of it. In the 1857 *Introduction,* Marx provides a clear answer to these questions. 'It seems to be correct', he says, 'to begin with the real and concrete', i.e. in the case of economics 'the population, which is the foundation and the subject of the entire social act of production.' Closer examination, however, shows that this fact achieves little towards a real, concrete knowledge. Whether we take the directly given totality itself, or the partial complexes of which it is composed, a knowledge that is oriented in this way towards the immediately given reality always ends up with merely notional ideas. These therefore have to be more exactly defined with the aid of isolating abstractions. This is in fact how the science of economics originally proceeded; it followed the path of abstraction ever further, until a genuine economic science arose, which based itself on the slowly acquired abstract elements. 'From there the journey would have to be retraced until I had finally arrived at the population again, but this time not as the chaotic conception of a whole, but as a rich totality of many determinations and relations.'³

In this way, the nature of the economic totality itself prescribes the paths towards its knowledge. But this correct procedure can still lead to idealist illusions, if the real independence of the existent is not constantly present to mind: the very process of knowledge itself, when isolated and treated as autonomous, contains within it the tendency to self-deception. Marx says of the synthesis that is obtained in this dual way: 'The concrete is concrete because it is the concentration of many determinations, hence unity of the diverse. It appears in the process of thinking, therefore, as a process of concentration, as a result, not as a point of departure, even though it is the point of departure in reality and hence also the point of departure for observation and conception.' The methodology that leads to Hegelian idealism can be deduced from this. The first path leads from the 'full conception' to 'abstract determinations', while along the second, 'the abstract determinations lead towards a reproduction of the concrete by way of thought. In this way Hegel fell into the illusion of conceiving the real as the product of thought concentrating itself, probing its own depths, and unfolding itself out of itself, by itself, whereas the method of rising from the abstract to the concrete is only the way in which thought appropriates the concrete, reproduces it as the concrete in the mind. But this is by no means the process by which the concrete itself comes into being.'⁴ The break with the idealist mode of conception is thus a double one. Firstly, it must be understood that the necessary path to knowledge which leads from the 'elements' obtained by abstraction towards knowledge of the concrete totality is simply a movement of knowledge and not that of reality itself. The latter consists of concrete and real interactions between these 'elements', within the actively or passively operative context of the composite totality. It follows from this that a change in the totality (and also in the

component partial totalities) can only be studied by investigating it as a process of real genesis. Inference by
deduction from categorical ideas easily leads, as the example
of Hegel shows, to unsupported speculative conceptions.

This does not of course mean that rational relationships
between the abstracted 'elements' are immaterial for the
knowledge of reality, even relationships of a process character.
On the contrary. It is just that we must never forget that
these elements, in their abstracted and generalized form, are
the product of thought, i.e. of knowledge. From the
ontological point of view, they are just as much complexes
of being in process, although their properties are simpler and
therefore easier to grasp than those of the total complex whose
'elements' they form. It is thus most important to discover
as precisely as possible the mode of their law-like functioning,
partly by empirical observation and partly by abstract thought
experiments, i.e. to see clearly what they are like in themselves, how their internal forces be ome effective, and what
interactions there are between them and other 'elements' when
disturbing factors are eliminated. It is clear, therefore, that
the 'retraced journey' that Marx describes as the method of
political economy presupposes a permanent collaboration
between historical (genetic) modes of thought and those that
reveal abstract and systematizing laws and tendencies. However, the organic and hence fruitful interaction between these
two paths to knowledge is only possible on the basis of a
permanent ontological criticism at every step, since these two
methods deal with the same real complexes and grasp them
from different aspects. Because of this, treatment in terms of
pure ideas can easily break the ontological correlations
between them, and ascribe these aspects a false autonomy,
either empirically historical or abstractly theoretical. Only an
uninterrupted and vigilant ontological criticism of that which
has been discovered as a fact or a relation, a process or a law,
can reestablish in thought a true insight into the phenomena.

Bourgeois economics continuously suffers from the duality resulting from the rigid separation of these perspectives. On the one hand it produces a purely empiricist economic history, in which the genuinely historical connection of the overall process vanishes; on the other hand, from the marginal utility theory through to the particular manipulative investigations of today, a science that can juggle away the genuine and decisive connections, in a sham theoretical way, even if it discovers by chance certain real relationships, or traces of these, in particular cases.

Secondly—and this is most closely connected with what has been said above—the opposition between 'elements' and totality should never be reduced to an opposition between the intrinsically simple and the intrinsically compound. Here the general categories of the whole and its parts receive an additional complication, without their being negated as a basic relationship. Every 'element' and every part, in other words, is just as much a whole; the 'element' is always a complex with concrete and qualitatively specific properties, a complex of various collaborating forces and relations. However, this complexity does not negate its character as an 'element'; the genuine categories of economics—precisely in their intricate, process-like and actual complexity, each in its own way and its own place—really are something 'final', which can be further analysed, but which can not be further decomposed in reality. The greatness of the founders of economics was particularly that they recognized this fundamental character of the genuine categories, and began to establish the correct relationships between them.

These relationships, however, are not simply juxtaposed, but contain a principle of super- and sub-ordination. It may seem that this contradicts what we were saying earlier, in polemicizing against the hierarchical principle of the idealist systems, and precisely indeed in the name of the Marxian ontology of social being. This contradiction is only apparent, although the appearance is significant, and is the source of many misunderstandings about Marxism. In particular, the principle of ontological priority must be clearly distinguished from the epistemological and moral, etc. value judgements which beset every idealist or vulgar materialist systemic hierarchy. If we ascribe one category ontological priority over the others, we simply mean that one of them can exist without the other, without the opposite being the case. This holds for the central thesis of all materialism, that being has ontological priority over consciousness. What this means ontologically is simply that there can be being without consciousness, while all consciousness must have something existent as its presupposition or basis. This does not involve any kind of value hierarchy between being and consciousness. Every concrete ontological investigation of their relationship shows rather that consciousness is only possible at a relatively high stage in the development of matter; modern biology is in the process of showing how what were originally physio-chemical modes of reaction of the organism to its environment gradually gave rise to ever more significant forms of consciousness, which moreover can only come to fruition at the stage of social being. It is just the same ontologically with the priority of the production and reproduction of human existence over other functions. If Engels, in his speech at Marx's graveside, spoke of the 'simple fact. . . that mankind must first of all eat, drink, have shelter and clothing, before it can pursue politics, science, art, religion, etc.'[5] , here again, it is exclusively ontological priority that is involved. Marx says this clearly himself in the Preface to *A Contribution to the Critique of Political Economy*. The most important thing here is that it is the 'sum total of relations of production' that Marx considers as the 'real foundation' from which forms of consciousness develop; these forms of consciousness are thus conditioned by the process of social, political and intellectual life. His conclusion, that 'It is not the consciousness of men that determines their being, but on the contrary their social being that determines their con-sciousness',[6] does not reduce the world of consciousness with its forms and contents directly to the economic structure, but rather relates it to the totality of social existence. The determination of consciousness by social being is thus meant in a quite general sense. It is only vulgar materialism (from the period of the Second International through to the Stalin period and its consequences) that made this into a unilateral and direct causal relationship between the economy, or even particular aspects of it, and ideology. Marx himself, however, directly before the ontologically decisive passage quoted above, says firstly that definite forms of social consciousness 'correspond' to the superstructure, and further that the mode of production of material life 'conditions' social, political and intellectual life in general.[7] Later on in this chapter, as well as in the second part of this work, we shall seek to show what a rich field of interactions and interrelations are included in this deliberately very general and open ontological determination, even in the context of the decisive Marxian category of the 'predominant moment.'

The erroneous conception of the Marxist method that is generally prevalent today has made this brief excursus necessary, and it has led us somewhat away from the central theme of our present investigation. If we return now to the method of economics itself, let us consider this in the highest and clearest form achieved by Marx, more particularly in *Capital*. (The *Grundrisse*, while it is full of instructive complexes and relations that are not analysed in *Capital*, still lacks in its overall composition the methodologically clear and ontologically fundamental new mode of presenta-tion of the completed master work.) If we attempt to define the decisive principles of its construction in a very general way, we could begin by saying that its point of departure involves a large-scale process of abstraction, from which a gradual path towards the comprehension in thought of the totality, in all its clear and richly articulated concreteness, is undertaken, by way of the resolution of the methodologically unavoidable abstractions.

Since a real isolation of individual processes by means of actual experiments is ontologically excluded in the area of social being, there can only be thought experiments of an abstractive character, which are employed to investigate theoretically how specific economic relations, connections, forces etc. work themselves out, when all the circumstances that block, inhibit and modify their validity in its pure form are excluded. Marx's great precursor, Ricardo, already embarked on this course, and in every later case that some kind of an economic theory has arisen, thought experiments of this kind play a similar eliminating role. But while thinkers such as Ricardo always proceeded on the basis of a sense for the living reality, a healthy instinct for the ontological, so that they always extracted real relationships between categories, even if these were often brought into false antinomies (the insuperable contradiction between law of value and rate of profit), the thought experiments of bourgeois economics generally have only a peripheral foundation in the real world (water in the Sahara in the marginal utility theory), which, by way of mechanical generalizations, orientation to the manipulation of detail, etc., rather detract from a knowledge of the overall process than point towards this. Marx is distinguished from the most significant of his forerunners particularly in a sense for reality that is heightened by having been made philosophically conscious, and this shows both in his comprehension of the dynamic totality and in his correct evaluation of the how and what of particular categories. This sense of reality, however, has a relevance beyond the limits of pure economics; no matter how bold the abstractions that Marx consistently elaborates within the strictly economic field, the life-giving interaction between the properly economic and the extra-economic reality is also continuously at work, in the context of the totality of social being, enabling the abstract theory to clarify theoretical questions that would otherwise remain insoluble.

This permanent ontological criticism and self-criticism in the Marxian doctrine of social being gives abstracting thought experiment in the area of pure economics a specific and epistemologically new character. The abstraction is firstly never a partial one, i.e. Marx never isolates one part or one 'element' in this abstraction, but rather the entire area of the economy appears in an abstracting projection, in which, as a result of the provisional exclusion in thought of certain more comprehensive categorical relationships, the categories that have been given a central place develop fully and undisturbed, and can reveal their internal lawfulness in pure forms. The abstraction of the thought experiment, on the other hand, still remains in constant touch with the totality of social being, including its extra-economic relations and tendencies, etc. This specific, seldom understood and paradoxically dialectical method is related to the already mentioned insight of Marx's to the effect that economic and extra-economic phenomena in social life continuously transform themselves into one another, and stand in an insuperable relationship of interaction; although, as has already been demonstrated, this leads neither to a lawless once-and-for-all historical development, nor to a mechanically 'law-like' rule of the abstract and purely economic. There is rather an organic unity of social being, with the role of the predominant moment, but no more, falling to the strict laws of economics.

This reciprocal mutual penetration of the economic and non-economic in social existence reaches deep into the doctrine of categories itself. Marx continues the work of classical economics, in so far as he fits wages into the general theory of value. He recognizes, however, that labour-power is a commodity *sui generis*, 'whose use-value possesses the peculiar property of being a source of value, whose actual consumption, therefore, is itself an embodiment of labour, and, consequently, a creation of value.'[8] Without going into the far-reaching consequences of this discovery at this point, we shall confine ourselves to the fact that this specific property of the commodity labour-power necessarily gives rise to a permanent intervention of extra-economic aspects in the operation of the law of value, even in the normal sale and purchase of this commodity. Whereas the value of other commodities is determined simply by the reproduction costs of the moment, 'there enters into the determination of the value of labour-power a historical and moral element.'[9] Finally,

'The nature of the exchange of commodities itself imposes no limit to the working-day, no limit to surplus-labour. The capitalist maintains his rights as a purchaser when he tries to make the working-day as long as possible, and to make, whenever possible, two working-days out of one. On the other hand, the peculiar nature of the commodity sold implies a limit to its consumption by the purchaser, and the labourer maintains his right as seller when he wishes to reduce the working-day to one of definite normal duration. There is here, therefore, an antinomy, right against right, both equally bearing the seal of the law of exchanges. Between equal rights force decides. Hence it is that in the history of capitalist production, the determination of what is a working-day, presents itself as the result of a struggle, a struggle between collective capital, i.e. the class of capitalists, and collective labour, i.e. the working class.'[10]

Extra-economic moments of this kind emerge with a necessity that is dictated by the law of value itself, and continuously, in the everyday life of capitalist commodity exchange, so to speak—the normal operation of the law of value. But after Marx has systematically analysed this world, with the necessary and closed character that its strict economic regularity endows it with, he devotes a separate chapter to its historical (ontological) genesis, and depicts the so-called 'primitive accumulation', a centuries-long chain of extra-economic acts of violence that was necessary to create for the first time the historical conditions that made labour-power into a specific commodity, and one that forms the foundation of the law-like character of the capitalist economy. '*Tantae molis erat,* to establish the "eternal laws of Nature" of the capitalist mode of production, to complete the process of separation .between labourers and conditions of labour, to transform, at one pole, the social means of production and subsistence into capital, at the opposite pole, the mass of the population into wage-labourers, into "free labouring poor", that artificial product of modern society.'[11]

It is only possible to understand the construction of *Capital* if attention is paid to the continuous interactions of this kind between the strictly law-like character of the economic, and the heterogenous relations, forces, etc. of the extra-economic: the construction of *Capital* leads from the experimental positing of purely law-like and abstractly homogenous relationships, via the successive insertion of wider components that are closer to reality, which occasionally leads to the negation of the original relationships, to finally arrive at the concrete totality of social being. Marx already provided in the 1857 *Introduction* a programme for the process of approximation and concretization that he undertook to accomplish in *Capital.* And even *Capital* itself remained incomplete; at the point where social classes become visible, as the result of the approximation to the concrete totality, the manuscript breaks off.* In order to culminate in this concrete way, research must begin with the 'elements' of central importance. For the path that Marx seeks to tread, from the abstract towards the concrete and thus comprehensible totality, can not take just any abstraction as its starting-point.

This is not just another case of the importance of the distinction that Marx stressed between appearance and essence. For if it is taken in isolation, any appearance whatsoever could be abstracted as an 'element' and made into the starting-point, even though a path of this kind would never lead to an understanding of the totality; the starting-point must rather be an objectively central category in the ontological sense.

This is the very reason why Marx in *Capital* investigates value as the first category, as the primary 'element', and particularly in the way that the genesis of this category presents itself. On the one hand this genesis shows abstractly, and reduced to one decisive moment, the most general outline of a history of the entire economic reality, while on the other hand the choice immediately demonstrates its fruitfulness, in so far as these categories themselves, together with the conditions and relationships that necessarily follow from their existence, clearly place in a central position the most important thing in the structure of social being, the social character of production. The genesis of value that Marx presents here immediately reveals the dual character of his method. This genesis itself is neither a logical deduction from the concept of value, nor an inductive description of the particular historical stages of its development up till the point at which it achieves its pure social form; it is rather a specific and novel synthesis which combines the historical ontology of social being theoretically and organically with the theoretical discovery of its concrete and actually effective regularities.

This introductory chapter does not claim to present the historical development of value in economic life *in extenso;* it simply gives the theoretically decisive steps in the self-movement of this category, from its initially sporadic and chance beginnings, up to the completed development in which its theoretical nature is expressed in pure form. This convergence of the historical-ontological and the theoretical stages of the emergence of the value category already shows its central place in the system of economic life. For, as we shall see below, it would be very hasty to conclude that the possibility opened here provided a general methodological foundation for the whole of economics, and to assume in general an overall parallel brooking no exception between theoretical and historical (ontological) development, between the succession and differentiation of economic categories. More than a few misunderstandings of the Marxian doctrine have their source in hasty generalizations of this kind, which were always foreign to Marx himself. It is only because in value, as the central category of social production, the most essential determinations that govern the overall process coincide, that the abbreviated ontological steps of the genesis of value, presented in a form that reduces them to their most decisive aspects, possess also a significance as the theoretical foundation of the concrete economic steps.

The central position of the value category is an ontological fact, and not a kind of 'axiom' that could serve as the point of departure for purely theoretical or even logical deductions. But once this ontological facticity is recognized, it already indicates something beyond its mere facticity; its theoretical analysis immediately shows it to be the focus of the most important tendencies of any social reality. Here, of course, we cannot even attempt to indicate the wealth of determinations involved in this. We shall just point out, as briefly as possibly, some of the most important aspects. First and foremost, the social category of value presents straight away the basic foundation of social existence, i.e. labour. Labour's connection with the social functions of value similarly reveals the fundamental structuring principles of social being that derive from the natural existence of human beings, and also from their metabolism with nature, a process in which every aspect—the inseparable ontological connection between the ultimately indestructible character of this material base and the continuous and constantly advancing conquest of it, both intensively and extensively, its transformation in the direction of pure sociality—shows a process that culminates in categories which, like value itself, have already completely cut loose from material nature.

For these reasons, an ontology of social being must always be governed by two perspectives. The first of these is that both poles, i.e. on the one hand objects that seem to belong directly and purely to nature (fruit trees, domestic animals, etc.), but which are in the last instance the products of human labour, and on the other hand social categories (above all value itself) which have already lost any natural materiality, must remain inseparably linked together in the dialectic of value. The very inseparability of use-value and exchange-value, which expresses itself as a contradiction, shows by its seemingly antithetical but still indissoluble connection, this ontological property of social being. The theoretical cul-de-sacs of bourgeois idealist social philosophy, which are continually re-emerging, very often originate in an abstract and antinomic contrast between the material and the mental, the natural and the social, which inevitably leads to the destruction of all genuine dialectical connections and thus makes the specific character of social being incomprehensible. (In the second part of this work we shall be able to go into this complex in more detail; for the time being we must just indicate the inseparability of the two poles.)

In the second place, this dialectic is also incomprehensible to anyone who does not manage to raise himself above the primitive view of the world which recognizes materiality, and even objective being, only in the form of actual things, and attributes all other forms of objectivity (connections, relationships, etc.), as well as all reflections of reality that directly appear as products of thought (abstractions, etc.), to a supposedly autonomous activity of consciousness. We have already discussed Hegel's attempts to overcome these conceptions, which are understandable in so far as they have a direct natural basis, but are nevertheless extremely primitive and in fact false from an objective standpoint.* The path-breaking character of the Marxian analysis of value is equally evident in Marx's treatment of abstraction. The changes undergone by labour in connection with the relation between use-value and exchange-value, which is ever more strongly developed, complete the transformation of concrete labour on a specific object into abstract, value-creating labour, culminating in the reality of socially necessary labour. If this process is considered free from the toils of idealist metaphysics, we must take note of the fact that this process of abstraction is a real process in the real social world. We have already shown in another context how the average character of labour already emerges, spontaneously and objectively, at a quite primitive stage of its social development, and that this is not a matter of mere knowledge independent of the ontological properties of its object, but rather the emergence of a new ontological category of labour itself in the course of its increasing socialization, which only much later is brought into consciousness. Socially necessary (and therefore *ipso facto* abstract) labour is also a reality, an aspect of the ontology of social being, an achieved real abstraction in real objects, quite independent of whether this is achieved by consciousness or not. In the nineteenth century, millions of independent artisans experienced the effects of this abstraction of socially necessary labour as their own ruin, i.e. they experienced in practice the concrete consequences, without having any suspicion that what they were facing was an achieved abstraction of the social process; this abstraction has the same ontological rigour of facticity as a car that runs you over.

It is similarly necessary to conceive connections and relationships ontologically. On this point Marx's presentation goes still further, at least polemically; he is not content simply to demonstrate that these connections and relationships are component parts of social being. He also shows that the unavoidable necessity of experiencing them as part of reality, and reckoning with their facticity in practical life, must often lead to transforming them in thought into things. We have already seen how the primitive mode of appearance of the ontological *'intentio recta'* can easily lead to a 'reification' of this kind of any existent in the human consciousness, and how this process finds a further extension and a fixation in thought in science and philosophy. In the celebrated chapter on the fetish character of commodities, Marx depicts in detail this process of 'reification' of social relations and relationships, and shows how this is not something confined to economic categories in the narrow sense, but provides the basis for an ontological distortion of the most subtle and important mental objects of an ever more social human life. Here Marx takes up again, at a more philosophically mature stage of his development, his criticism of the Hegelian concepts of externalization and alienation. This indication must suffice here, as a special chapter will be devoted to this question in the second part.

To go back to the overall construction of the first volume of *Capital*, we see that the immanent complex of the contradictions of value, which is something inherent in the thing itself, gives rise to a broader and more mature development of the most crucial economic categories. We have already indicated certain general problems of labour; before we go on to deal with these again, we must say something about the development of money from the general form of value. If Marx's analysis of value ends up with money as the necessary, 'logical' consequence, the ontological sense of this 'logical' should not be taken literally, and thus reduced to a matter of thought. It should be clearly seen, rather, that what is involved here is primarily a question of ontological necessity, and that Marx's 'deduction', therefore, only appears as a logical deduction on account of the abstractly abbreviated form, reduced to the most general characteristics, in which it is presented. In fact, however, it is the theoretical content of factual relationships that is sought here, and Marx himself stresses in his Afterword to the Second Edition of *Capital* that the appearance of an '*a priori* construction' is simply a function of the method of presentation, rather than that of inquiry.[12] Here again, Marx stresses the priority of the ontological, if certainly an ontological principle that is based on a strictly scientific methodology; the role of philosophy is then 'simply' that of a continuous ontological control and criticism, and, in places, also a role of broader and deeper generalization.

This function of philosophical generalization in no way weakens the scientific exactness of the particular economic-theoretical analyses, it 'simply' places them in those relationships that are indispensable for the adequate understanding of social being in its totality. We have just brought up a question of this kind with the problem of 'reification', though Marx in no way confines himself to this problem alone. For it is possible for a strictly scientific presentation of the ontological genesis of value, money, etc., if this is restricted to one particular science alone, to give the false appearance that the actual course of history has a purely rational character, which would be to falsify its ontological nature. It is true that a pure, law-like rationality of this kind is not only the nature of particular economic processes, but, at least tendentially, that of the overall economic process itself. But it should never be forgotten that although these law-like characteristics are syntheses, which arise in the real world itself out of the practical economic acts performed by individuals, who are conscious of them as such, yet their ultimate results, which are what is fixed in the theory, go far beyond the powers of theoretical comprehension and practical decision of the individuals who carry out these practical acts. It is thus quite regular for the results of particular economic acts carried out by men themselves in their practice (and with a practical consciousness of these), to assume the form of appearance of a transcendent 'destiny' even for the actors themselves. This is what happens in the case of 'reification' already referred to, and it is particularly striking in the case of money. Marx 'deduced' the genesis of money, from the dialectic of value, in a rationally legitimate, or one might say logically rigorous, way. Money as it thus necessarily arises as the product of human activity nevertheless intrudes into human society as something that is not understood, is inimical, and destroys all sacred ties, and it maintained this power, whose secret was not suspected, for thousands of years. In the *Economic and Philosophical Manuscripts* Marx compiled a few particularly important poetic expressions of this feeling.[13]

Of course this is not just a matter of money. What is revealed here is the basic structure of the relation between social theory and practice. It is one of the epoch-making merits of Marx's doctrine that he discovered the priority of practice, its guiding and controlling function for knowledge. But he was not simply content to explain this fundamental relationship in general, but also pointed out the methods for revealing the way in which this adequate relation of theory and practice came into social existence. And it is evident in this connection that any practice, even the most direct and everyday, can be seen to have this connection in relation to understanding, consciousness, etc., because it is always a teleological act, in which the projection of goals precedes their realization, both actually and chronologically. This in no way means that knowledge of the social consequences of a particular act is only possible in so far as this is a partial cause of a change in social being in its totality (or partial totality). Human social and economic action releases forces, tendencies, objectivities, structures, etc. that arise exclusively as a result of human practice, even though their nature may remain completely or in large part incomprehensible to those responsible. Thus Marx says of one particular kind of elementary everyday fact, i.e. that the connection of products of labour as values arises from simple exchange, 'We are not aware of this, nevertheless we do it.'[14] Thus the essence of this practice has to be grasped not only at the level of immediate practice, but also where theory is involved. Marx points out in the case of Benjamin Franklin's attempts to discover value in labour, 'But although ignorant of this, yet he says it.'[15] Points of this kind are of fundamental importance for the economic and its history, and for economic theory and its history, but, in the gradual transition from science to philosophy, they reach beyond the realm of the economic and apply to everything that happens in social being and in consciousness in this respect. Here again the ontological genesis demonstrates its all-embracing scope. If this relationship between practice and consciousness is established in the elementary facts of everyday practical life, then the phenomena of reification, alienation, the fetishization of a misunderstood reality into a self-created counterfeit, no longer appear as puzzling expressions of unknown and unconscious forces within or outside of man, but rather as mediations that are sometimes very widespread in the most elementary practice itself. (The problems arising here can also only be discussed in detail in the second part.)

Marx's presentation of the two specific and qualitatively distinct commodities, money and labour-power, provides in full detail a closed and seemingly complete picture of the first truly social production, i.e. capitalism, together with continuous glances back at more primitive economic formations, the elaboration of the differences serving primarily to throw light on this specifically social character of capitalist production, its substantial and categorical overcoming of the 'natural boundary', from as many sides as possible. Without even beginning to touch on the wealth of detail in *Capital,* we should point out that Marx, in so far as he investigated the development of any complex of facts or any category from the standpoint of its growth into a purely social one, provided the basis for an ontological theory of the development of social being. It is very fashionable today to laugh condescendingly at ideas of progress, and to make use of the contradictions that necessarily arise with every development in order to render any idea of progress, i.e. any development from an ontologically lower stage to a higher one, scientifically disreputable as a subjective value judgement. Yet the ontological investigation of social being shows that its categories and relations only very gradually, and by very many steps, attained a predominantly social character. We stress the word 'predominantly', for it is precisely the nature of social being that it can never cut itself completely loose from its basis in nature—man remains insuperably a biological being—just as organic nature has to incorporate inorganic in a transcended form. Social being, however, involves a development in which these natural categories, although they never disappear, nevertheless retreat ever more into the background in relation to the leading role of categories that can never have any analogy in nature. This is what happens in commodity exchange, where certain forms that are close to nature (cattle as a general means of exchange) are replaced by the purely social form of money; similarly, absolute surplus-value still has certain 'natural' components to it, whereas relative surplus-value, which has arisen from the growth of productivity that reduces the value of labour-power, already involves a form of exploitation in which surplus-value and hence exploitation can increase even in the context of an increase in wages. A similar thing, again, happened in the industrial revolution, when man and his faculties ceased to be the decisive factors in labour, and human labour itself came to be disanthropomorphized, etc.

All lines of development of this kind have an ontological character, i.e. they show in what direction, and with what changes in objectivity, connections and relationships, etc., the decisive categories of economics ever more clearly over-came their originally predominant natural ties, and assumed ever more decisively a predominantly social character. There are of course also categories that arise with a purely social character. This is already the case with value, although because of its inseparability from use-value, this is in a certain respect tied to a natural basis, even if one that has been socially transformed. There can be no doubt that a development is involved here, and just as little doubt that a progression can be established, from a purely ontological standpoint, in so far as this new form of social being increasingly comes into its own in the course of the developmental process, i.e. it is achieved more and more in independent categories, and increasingly maintains its natural forms only in a transcended way. An ontological establishment of progress of this kind does not involve any kind of subjective value judgement. It is the establishment of an ontological situation that exists no matter how it is evaluated. (The 'retreat of the natural boundary' can be either acclaimed or lamented.)

Despite the correctness of all this, it would be economic objectivism to remain at this point, and Marx does not stop here. But he goes beyond this along objective ontological paths, and not those of subjective evaluation, in so far as he presents the dynamic interaction between the economic categories and the objects and forces of social being as a whole—naturally these interactions find their centre in the focal point of this being, in man. But even this place of man in the totality of social being is an objective ontological one, quite free of any subjective evaluation of the complex of problems that arise in these processes. This ontological perspective is based on Marx's penetrating conception of appearance and essence in the process-like totality of social being. Marx's clearest statement of these questions is to be found—and not at all by chance—in his polemic against those who assess this development from a subjective, moral or cultural-philosophical standpoint, etc. We can take the contrast between Sismondi and Ricardo that Marx makes in *Theories of Surplus-Value*. In defence of the objective economist Ricardo, Marx says: 'Production for its own sake means nothing but the development of human productive forces, in other words the *development of the richness of human nature as an end in itself. . .*' The 'unedifying reflections' of Sismondi 'reveal a failure to understand the fact that, although at first the development of the capacities of the *human* species takes place at the cost of the majority of human individuals and even classes, in the end it breaks through this contradiction and coincides with the development of the individual; the higher development of individuality is thus only achieved by a historical process during which individuals are sacrificed. . .'[16] The fact that the development of the productive forces is referred back to that of the human species is in no way a renunciation of the objective ontological standpoint. Marx simply supplements the objectively given picture of the development of the productive forces in the economy with a picture that is essentially just as objective of the consequences of this economic development for the men in question (who bring it about in practice). And in indicating the contradiction that is just as objectively present, that the higher development of the human species is only brought about at the cost of whole classes of men, Marx still remains on the ground of an ontology of social being, in which connection it clearly emerges that the essence of the ontological development consists in the economic progress (ultimately affecting the destiny of the human species), and that the ontologically necessary and objective contradictions involved in this are its forms of appearance.

Later on in this chapter we shall come on to speak of the further development of the complex relationship of complexes, which reaches right through to the seemingly distant problems of ethics, aesthetics, etc., which are in reality complicated by many mediations. But even leaving this aside for the time being, the pattern of the first volume of *Capital* remains highly paradoxical, both in its content and methodology. Again and again, the strict and exact scientifically economic analysis opens out perspectives of an ontological kind on the totality of social being. This unity expresses the underlying tendency in Marx of developing philosophical generalizations out of the facts established by way of scientific research and methods, i.e. thorough ontological foundation of both scientific and philosophical assertions. This unity of solidly based fact and bold philosophical generalization is what gives Marx's *Capital* its extremely lively atmosphere.

A fundamental aspect of the whole edifice fades or even disappears for the reader who is not versed in theory, i.e. the premise of economic abstraction: the abstraction that all commodities are bought and sold at their value. This is moreover an abstraction *sui generis:* it is based on the real basic law of commodity exchange in society, a law that is ultimately always at work, through all the fluctuations of price, in the normally functioning totality. Hence its effect, both in the discovery of purely economic relationships, as well as in their inter-relation with extra-economic facts and tendencies of social being, is not that of an abstraction, and the entire first volume of *Capital* appears as a picture of the real world, not as an abstracting thought experiment. Once again, the root lies in the ontological character of this abstraction. It means no more and no less than the isolating accentuation of the basic law in commodity exchange, giving this undisturbed and un-inhibited validity, without it being weakened or modified by other structural relationships and processes that are necessarily also at work in a society of this kind. For this reason, this abstracting reduction to the most essential enables all aspects, economic as well as extra-economic, to appear undistorted, whereas an abstraction not ontologically founded or oriented to something peripheral would necessarily lead to the misrepresentation of the decisive categories. This shows once more the essential point of the new method: the manner and direction of the abstractions and thought experiments are not determined by epistemological or methodological (and least of all logical) standpoints, but by the thing itself, i.e. the ontological nature of the material in question.

The very construction of *Capital* shows that Marx is dealing with an abstraction, for all the evidence adduced from the real world. The composition of *Capital* proceeds by way of the successive integration of new ontological elements and tendencies into the world originally depicted on the basis of this abstraction, and the scientific investigation of the new categories, tendencies and relationships that arise from this, until finally the entire economy as the primary dynamic centre of social being is encompassed in thought before our eyes. The next step that has to be taken here leads to the overall process itself, initially conceived in a general way. For even though the whole society always forms the background to Volume One of *Capital,* the central theoretical presentations only grasp individual acts, even when dealing with such things as a whole factory with many workers, with a complex division of labour, etc. Later on the individual processes that have been previously considered separately have to be dealt with from the standpoint of the entire society. Marx repeatedly stresses that the first thing is an abstract and therefore formal presentation of the phenomena. In this connection, for example, 'the bodily form of the commodities produced was quite immaterial for the analysis', for the abstract laws apply in the same way to any kind of commodity. It is only the fact that the sale of one good (C-M) in no way necessarily leads to the purchase of another (M-C), that indicates the distinctness of the overall process from the individual acts, in the form of an insuperable contingency. It is only when the overall process is investigated from the standpoint of its law-like character, which affects the economy as a whole, that this formal comprehension is no longer sufficient: 'The re-conversion of one portion of the value of the product into capital and the passing of another portion into the individual consumption of the capitalist as well as the working class form a movement within the value of the product itself in which the result of the aggregate capital finds expression; and this move-ment is not only a replacement of value, but also a replace-ment in material and is therefore as much bound up with the relative proportions of the value-components of the total social product as with their use-value, their material shape.'[17]

This particular problem, which is of course a central one, already indicates that the path from the individual processes to the overall process in no way involves any further level of abstraction, as would seem to be supposed by modern habits of thought, but on the contrary a cancellation of certain limitations of the abstraction, the beginning of an approxima-tion to the concreteness of the conceived totality. It goes without saying that here, too, we can not undertake a detailed summary of the second volume of *Capital;* all we can do is to illustrate the most important basic problems of this stage from the standpoint of their ontological importance. The overall process of economic reproduction is the unity of three processes with three different levels: the circuits of money capital, of productive capital and of commodity capital are its component parts. Once again, we must stress at the outset that here, too, it is not a question of dissecting a process purely methodologically, but rather that three real economic processes actually combine into one united process;

the conceptual dissection is no more than a reflection in thought of three processes of reproduction: of industrial capital, commercial capital and money capital. (The problems associated with this are made more concrete in the third volume of *Capital*.) The content, elements, stages and succession of the three processes are in all cases the same. Their essential distinction, however, is where they begin, and where they cease once the particular process of reproduction is concluded. The continuity of the process of social reproduction is certainly not negated here. On the one hand, every ending is equally the beginning of a new circuit, while on the other hand, the three processes are intertwined together and their unitary movement is what forms the overall process of reproduction. 'If we combine all three forms, all premises of the process appear as its result, as a premise produced by it itself. Every element appears as a point of departure, of transit, and of return. The total process presents itself as the unity of the processes of production and circulation. The process of production becomes the mediator of the process of circulation and vice versa... The reproduction of capital in each one of its forms and stages is just as continuous as the metamorphosis of these forms and the successive passage through the three stages. The entire circuit is thus really a unity of its three forms.'[18]

The analysis of these circuits results in the most important proportional relation of capitalist society, destroys without a great deal of polemic the immediate idea of capital as a 'thing-like' objectivity, and shows capital as a relation, whose specific mode of existence is an uninterrupted process. So that the proportionalities arising here appear quite transparently, Marx carries out a new abstraction to replace the abstractions of the first volume, in so far as he selects as a starting-point simple reproduction without accumulation, in order to use the knowledge obtained from this to go on to deal with true reproduction, reproduction on an extended scale. To assess

Marx's method correctly, it must be stressed that here, too, the abstraction in question is one that itself forms part of the real world, and which thus provides a basis for reflecting the real process in its true determinations, even though this later needs supplementing, just as did the abstraction of the first volume. 'As far as accumulation does take place, simple reproduction is always a part of it, and can therefore be studied by itself, and is an actual factor of accumulation.'[19]

In the transition to reproduction on an extended scale, Marx gives up this abstraction, but there still remains the abstraction, in relation to the real process, that no attention is paid to the increase in productivity.

This is all the more striking, in so far as when the abstractions are abandoned in the third volume, this problem is constantly treated as an autonomous aspect of the concrete theory of the overall process. (We shall come back to this below in considering the average rate of profit.) It is of course possible that Marx's views on this point will become clear when the entire text of *Capital* is published. But whether this is so or not, it is at least worth devoting some attention to this problem, since it makes it clear how Marx's economics can be employed to provide knowledge of the social being of a period after his own. It remains true, in particular, that the insertion of the increase of productivity into the analysis of the overall process is not necessarily different, from the ontological standpoint, from the transition from simple reproduction to reproduction on an extended scale, no matter how significant are the new characteristics that come into view. The remark by Marx that was quoted above also applies to this new question, even supposing that the insertion of increasing productivity introduces a new dimension into the actual content of relationships.[20] The ontological foundation in Marx's method of abstraction is precisely what makes further concretization of this kind possible, without the methodological basis having to be changed even in the slightest respect. (This of course applies only to the method of Marx himself. False abstractions by his followers in the spirit of the modern specific sciences have a completely different character, for example the theory of so-called 'absolute immiseration' in the version put forward by Kautsky.)

The concrete economic analysis of the so-called schemas of overall reproduction given in the second volume does not really belong here. It should only be stressed that the proportions that arise in this connection are always concrete and qualitatively specific complexes. Naturally the proportions themselves can most clearly be expressed in quantitative terms, but they are always proportions of qualitatively specific complexes; the fact that the major division is that between means of production and means of consumption, and that the relations between constant capital in the one department and variable capital in the other show a quantitative proportionality, already shows that the quantitative value proportions must contain within them in an insuperable way the qualitatively different use-values to which they are ontologically linked. This is one of the inadvertible consequences of the concretization involved in the transition from the first volume to the second. We have already indicated the general problem. All that still has to be emphasized here is that in the production process, as an aspect of the general circulation, the inseparable dialectical connection between use-value and exchange-value emerges in two ways: naturally, on the one hand, at the conclusion of each step, since a use-value is indispensably necessary in order to realize an exchange-value; but also at the beginning of each step, when the capitalist, in order to produce, has to provide himself with the necessary means of production and the labour-power to put them in motion; he buys both these two factors for the sake of their use-value in production. This may seem to be a commonplace, and it is so far the 'intentio recta' of ordinary everyday practice. But then a pseudo-theoretical generalization is made, as it is by bourgeois economics with its conceptually vacuous abstraction M-M' (money at the beginning and end of the reproduction process). And the economics of the Stalin era, which called itself Marxist, considered the theory of value simply as a theory that showed how exchange-value functioned. It is not superfluous in the interest of reestablishing the genuine Marxism to stress that the ontologically valid '*intentio recta*' forms the foundation of science and philosophical generalization, and that no economic phenomenon can be correctly understood without proceeding from the relationships present in reality itself—in this case from the ontological inseparability of use-value and exchange-value, even in their mutual opposition.

It is the approach to concrete properties of social being that results from the comprehension of the reproduction process in its totality, that gives Marx the possibility of further dispensing with the initial abstractions. This occurs in the theory of the rate of profit. Value and surplus-value still remain the basic ontological categories of the capitalist economy. At the level of abstraction of the first volume, it suffices to establish that only the specific property of the commodity labour-power is able to create a new value, whereas means of production, raw materials, etc. merely retain their value in the course of the labour process. The concretization of the second volume provides an analysis of the overall process, in many respects still on the same basis, in so far as constant capital, variable capital and surplus-value figure as elements in the circulation process. Here the fact comes into play that in the general process—considered purely in its generality, thus deliberately abstracted methodologically from the individual acts that compose it—the law of value retains its validity unaltered. This again is an ontologically correct and important fact, for the deviations from the law of value necessarily cancel each other out in the totality. In terms of a simple formula, consumption (including the productive consumption of the society) cannot possibly be greater than production). As an abstraction, this naturally presupposes that foreign trade is omitted from consideration; correctly, since it is quite possible here, without any further ado, to cancel this abstraction again, and to take account of the resulting variations in the complex of laws; we can point out in passing that this whole problem disappears when the theory is applied to the world economy as a whole.

We now come up against the problem of the third volume: on the basis of the overall circulation process, to investigate the laws that regulate individual economic acts, and now not only in isolation, but in the context of the overall process. This effect of the individual acts on the overall process, which modifies the categories ontologically, rests on two real historical assumptions: on the one hand the growth of the productive forces with their value-reducing effect, on the other, the widespread possibility for capital to be moved from one field to another. Both of these factors presuppose a relatively high level of development of social production, which shows moreover that economic categories, in their pure and developed form, require a developed existence in the mode of functioning of social being, i.e. that their categorical development, their categorical overcoming of the natural boundary, is a product of the social-historical development.

But even under these circumstances, the formation of the rate of profit as a determining economic category is neither a mechanical law independent of human economic activity, nor the direct product of this activity. The transformation of surplus-value into profit, and of the rate of surplus-value into the profit rate, is of course a methodological consequence of the cancellation, in the third volume, of the abstractions of the first. Even here, as we have seen in the case of all these abstractions of Marx and the concretizations that supersede them, surplus-value remains the foundation; it simply leads to a further relationship that is equally real, and remains dependent on the original one. Whereas surplus-value is related only to the value of labour-power, hence to the variable capital that puts this into operation in a capitalist sense, profit, which is directly—though only directly—identical with surplus-value in a quantitative sense, is also related to constant capital. The separate acts that constitute production, circulation, etc. are therefore primarily oriented towards the increase of profit. The development of the productive forces, a phenomenon which necessarily first appears in particular places, now produces in these cases an additional profit, which naturally becomes the goal of the teleological acts of the individual producers; for a decrease in the value of the product that is achieved in this way enables the commodity to be sold above its value, while still more cheaply than it is sold by other producers. When a stage of development is reached which permits capital to be shifted from one field to another more or less at will, the former phenomenon does not lead to any lasting monopoly, but rather to a reduction in the price corresponding to the largest decline in value effected by increased productivity. Thus the possibility of this movement of capital produces on the one hand an average rate of profit, while on the other hand this movement gives rise to a tendency for the rate of profit to fall, precisely as a result of the growth of the productive forces.

The exact way in which Marx depicts the tendential character of this new law is a purely economic problem which we need not go into here. All that our particular purpose requires us to establish is, firstly, that the tendency, as the necessary form of appearance of a law in the concrete totality of social being, is a necessary product of the fact that real complexes are involved with other real complexes in complicated and often very indirect reciprocal relationships; the tendency character of the law is the expression of its essential nature as the resultant of this kind of dynamic movement of complexes, full of contradictions. In the second place, we note that although the falling rate of profit tendency is certainly the end product of individual teleological acts, and therefore conscious projects, its content and direction, etc. produce the very opposite of that which is aimed at, both objectively and subjectively, in these acts. This elementary and necessary basic condition of social and historical human existence and activity appears here in a precisely controllable and factual form; once economic relationships are conceived in their dynamic and concrete totality, it is clear again and again that although men certainly make their own history, yet the results of the historical course are different, and often the opposite, from what the human will, which can be eliminated neither as an individual nor as a general factor, intends. It is also the case here that the phenomenon of an objective progress emerges within the overall movement. The fall in the rate of profit presupposes a change in the value of products as a consequence of a decline in the labour socially necessary to produce them. This has the further meaning of a rise in man's domination of natural forces, in his capabilities, and a decline in the labour-time socially necessary for production.

The other great complex involved in the dissolution of abstractions and establishment of concrete complexes in the third volume, is the social distribution of the surplus-value become profit. In the abstractions of the first and second volumes, there are simply industrial capitalists and workers confronting one another. Even where commercial and money capital appear to be involved in the circulation process, in Volume Two, it is only their place in the overall movement that is depicted, and this is still regulated by the as yet undifferentiated categories of value and surplus-value. It is only in Volume Three that commercial and money capital (as well as ground rent), assume their concrete role in the distribution of profits. Even here, the ontological priority of surplus-value as previously depicted in its single rule, proves itself to be unsurpassable, since this is the only point at which new value arises; surplus-value that is transformed into profit is now distributed between all the representatives of the social division of labour that are economically necessary, even though they do not create any new value, and the analysis of this process, which we cannot go into here in detail, is what constitutes the essential part of Volume Three. It must still be noted, however, that it is this concretization of all the active factors of economic life that makes possible the transition from economics in the narrower sense, to the class division, without discontinuity in the social articulation. (Here, unfortunately, we have only a few introductory lines of Marx. Methodologically, however, the path ahead is quite clear.)

It follows from this that the third volume also contains the longest and most detailed excursus on the history of the economic complex newly emerging here. Without this, commercial and money capital, as well as ground rent, could not be fitted into the general arrangement of the whole economy. Their historical genesis is the prerequisite for a theoretical understanding of their present efficacy in the system of a genuinely social production, although (or precisely because) this historical derivation cannot by itself explain the role they eventually undertook. This is determined rather by their subordination to industrial production, even though they existed independently long before, and, despite a certain constant specificity, fulfilled completely different economic and social functions. It is evident in this connection that the majority of derivations of the genesis of value given here display very disparate characteristics. The demonstration that all these, taken together, result in a unified picture of historical development, leads back to the problems of the general Marxist theory of history, which our earlier discussions already constantly touched on. But before we go on to discuss this, we must once again direct our attention to the analysis of categories in the Introduction to the *Grundrisse,* where the complexity and dynamic of categorical structures and relationships may give us a broader and firmer basis for tackling the historical problems.

Marx discusses here the general relationship of production to consumption, distribution, etc. It is a commonplace that the Marxist ontology of social being assigns priority to production, but one that, for all its general correctness, has been overstretched in a vulgarizing way that has frequently hindered the understanding of Marx's real method, and led people onto false paths. This priority must be characterized more closely, and Marx's concept of the predominant moment in the field of complex interactions must be understood more exactly.

The question here is that of the most general and fundamental categories of economics—production, consumption, distribution, exchange and circulation. The bourgeois economics of Marx's time in part identified these categories (e.g. production and consumption), in part made exclusive oppositions out of them, and in part established false hierarchies between them. Marx deals particularly with the Hegelian variant of these false relationships, which sought—with the aid of the logical categories of generality, particularity and singularity—to fit them into a syllogism. Marx remarks, 'This is admittedly a coherence, but a shallow one', and shows that the logical apparatus that produced the syllogism could only be based on superficial and abstract characteristics. He appends a short polemic against those bourgeois supporters or opponents of the political economists 'who accuse them of barbarically tearing apart things which belong together'. Marx retorts, again in the name of a rejection of a treatment of relationships in terms of logical definition, that these relationships have an existential, ontological character: 'As if this rupture had made its way not from reality into the textbooks, but rather from the textbooks into reality, and as if the task were the dialectic[al] balancing of concepts, and not the grasping of real relations!'[21] Marx takes up just as decisive a position against the Hegelian standpoint that sees production and consumption as identical. The 'socialist belletrists' and vulgar economists who represent this point of view fall into the error of considering 'society as one single subject', i.e. wrongly and speculatively.[22] Here as on so many other occasions, Marx warns against making the irreducible, dialectical and contradictory unity of society, a unity that emerges as the end product of the interaction of innumerable heterogenous processes, into an intrinsically homogenous unity, and impeding adequate knowledge of this unity by inadmissable and simplifying homogenizations of this kind. We may add that whether this homogenization is speculative or positivist, it amounts to the same thing in this respect.

Marx goes on to analyse the real interrelations, starting with the most complicated case, the relation between production and consumption. Here, as also in the other articulations, the ontological aspect is brought to the fore, i.e. that all these categories, even though they may stand in very intricate mutual relations to one another, are 'forms of being, characteristics of existence', that they therefore form a totality, and can only be scientifically understood as existing elements and moments of this totality. Two things follow from this. Firstly, each element retains its ontological specificity, and reveals this in all its interactions with other categories, which also means that there can not be any general logical forms for these relations, but that each must be understood in its characteristic specificity; secondly, these interrelations are not of equal value, either pair by pair or as a whole, but they are rather all pervaded by the ontological priority of production as the predominant moment. If we thus consider the relationship of production and consumption, basing ourselves on these insights, then it is clear that we have a relationship of a kind very close to what Hegel treated as the reflection determination. This methodological kinship shows itself in the fact that the reciprocal relation constantly presents itself at the level of understanding always as an abstract identity, or as just as abstract a distinction in the appearance, and that the two viewpoints can only be transcended in the rational view of concrete interactions. Yet this is purely a methodological affinity. In Marx, it is the aspect of being that dominates; these characteristics are real aspects of real, and really dynamic complexes, and it is only on the basis of this dual ontological character (being in reciprocal interrelations and complex connection as well as within this specific being) that their relationship of reflection can be understood. In the materialist dialectic, in the dialectic of the thing itself, a development of really existing, and often heterogenous tendencies, appears as a contradictory correlation of the pair of categories. The rejection of merely logical determinations, in order to return to the ontological its true significance, thus represents an extraordinary concretization of the two-in-one relation.

Marx summarizes this situation on the basis of production in such a way that production determines the object, mode and aim of consumption. The first aspect is immediately comprehensible. The second opens up very extensive perspectives on the whole of human life. Marx says on this point: '*Firstly*, the object is not an object in general, but a specific object which must be consumed in a specific manner, to be mediated in its turn by production itself. Hunger is hunger, but the hunger gratified by cooked meat eaten with a knife and fork is a different hunger from that which bolts down raw meat with the aid of hand, nail and tooth. Production thus produces not only the object but also the manner of consumption, not only objectively but also subjectively.' This function of production is even more clearly visible in the third aspect. The ontological historic character of this relation is already shown in the fact that Marx connects its efficacy with the emergence of consumption 'from its initial state of natural crudity and immediacy', i.e. with a stage at which the genuine humanization of man, the tendency for the autonomous constitution of the categories of social being, is proclaimed. The general tendency of consumption for the need to be mediated and modified by the object, here reveals for the first time its essentially social character. In itself, this mediation is abstractly present even in the natural state, and at the stage where natural characteristics still predominate, but the relation of the object to the need at this stage remains constant, in such a way that the need can completely, or at least predominantly, retain its nature-like and instinctive character. It is only when, as the result of production, that object is subjected to a change—even if this is to begin with extremely gradual—that the new relationship emerges: the shaping of the need by the object as a process. What is involved here is a social relationship of a universal kind: naturally, it is primarily accomplished in material production, but it necessarily extends to take hold of productivity of any kind, no matter how mediated or how intellectual in character. As Marx stresses in this connection, 'The object of art—like every other product—creates a public which is sensitive to art and enjoys beauty. Production thus not only creates an object for the subject, but also a subject for the object.'[23]

The analysis of the relationship of consumption to production also produces important reciprocities, which are similarly indispensable to the existence and functioning of the productive process. In particular, that production is only genuinely accomplished in consumption; without consumption, all production would be mere possibility, and ultimately purposeless, hence non-existent in the social sense. It becomes more concrete in the further reciprocal determination that consumption 'creates the motive for production; it also creates the object which is active in production as its determinant aim'. As we shall see later on in detail, this means that it is through consumption that the essential content of the teleological project which sets production in motion and governs it, is determined; more precisely, 'that consumption *ideally posits* the object of production as an internal image, as a need, as drive and as purpose.'[24] We thus see that the interaction is many-sided and intertwined in many ways; we also see, however, that the basic condition of the materialist dialectic comes into its own in this richly articulated relationship of reflection determinations: there is no real interaction (no real reflection determination) without a predominant moment. If this underlying relationship is neglected, then we get either a one-sided and hence mechanical causal sequence which falsifies and simplifies the phenomena, or else a superficially scintillating but direction-less interaction, whose meaninglessness Hegel already correctly criticized, though of course without finding a solution. In the case of the interaction between production and consumption, it is clear that the former 'is the real point of departure and hence also the predominant moment'.[25] It is precisely because this last result of the analysis of economic categories was conceived as the central question of the Marxian method, without the ontological presuppositions of these categories being respected, that it was an absolute necessity to show that this truth collapses into falsehood if it is applied to social being without its presuppositions and their implications for the economy.

If we come now to consider the second most important relationship, that of production and distribution, somewhat more closely, we are confronted here by problems of a completely different kind. What is ultimately involved here, in the last instance, is the connection between purely economic forms, and the social and historical world which we characterized in our preceding discussions as the extra-economic. If this is neglected, as there are strong tendencies towards in vulgar Marxism, then Marxism is reduced to an 'economism', a restricted 'individual science' in the bourgeois sense. Whether this is then radically followed through in a one-sided way, or whether it is 'supplemented' by other individual sciences—out of epistemological considerations—does not make any essential difference. In both cases it results in a break with the ontological unity and specificity of social being, and hence with the unitary dialectical materialist science and philosophy as the most suitable method of comprehending it. By elaborating the connections between production and distribution, Marx brings the dialectical opposition of the economic and extra-economic into an organic and law-like relationship with the science of economics; in particular, this involved a break with the generally dominant vulgar conception of distribution. In this, distribution appeared simply as the distribution of products, and therefore seemed completely independent of production. 'But before distribution can be the distribution of products, it is: (1) the distribution of the instruments of production, and (2), which is a further specification of the same relation, the distribution of the members of the society among the different kinds of production. (Subsumption of the individuals under specific relations of production.) The distribution of products is evidently only a result of this distribution, which is composed within the process of production itself and determines the structure of production.'[26]

The false appearance corresponds to the viewpoint of the individual, who is directly subject here to the operation of a social law that determines his position in society, in production. A similar appearance exists also for the society as a whole, in so far as certain historical events, such as conquests, can in certain circumstances reform or transform the relations of distribution in the above Marxian sense. There is no question but that, in cases of this kind, conquest frequently gives rise to a new distribution. Either the conquered people are subjected to the production conditions of the victors, or else the mode of production is made more severe by means of tribute, or finally the interaction may lead to something new. All these variants seem attributable purely to extra-economic forces. Concrete examination shows, however, that the developmental tendency of the underlying relations of production always determines the way in which these reciprocal relations between distribution conditions that have arisen from extra-economic reasons work themselves out, so that production plays the role of the predominant moment. Whatever may be the immediate relations of pure power, the fact remains that the men who represent these or who are subjected to them are men who have to reproduce their own life under definite concrete conditions, who accordingly possess definite aptitudes, skills, abilities, etc., and who can only behave and adapt accordingly. So if a new distribution of the population takes place from extra-economic power relations, then this is never independent of the economic inheritance of the past developments, and a durable settlement of the future economic relations necessarily arises from an interaction between the human groups who are stratified in this way. If Marx attributes the function of the predominant moment in such interrelations to the mode of production, we must avoid understanding this in the sense of an economist practicism or utilitarianism. The mode of behaviour determined by production can even have a destructive character, as Marx shows in his examples of the devastations of the Mongolian hordes in Russia. But even this kind of behaviour refers back to the relations of production, to the pastoralism that required above all large uninhabited expanses. Finally in this connection Marx speaks of pillage as the mode of life of certain primitive peoples. 'But, for pillage to be possible, there must be something to be pillaged, hence production.'[27]

We see then that production as the predominant moment is understood here in the widest (ontological) sense, as the production and reproduction of human life, which even at very primitive levels (Mongolian cattle-raising) goes far beyond mere biological maintenance and must have a definite socio-economic character. It is this general form of production that determines distribution in the Marxian sense. To put it more precisely: it is a question of the men whose abilities, customs, etc. make certain modes of production possible; these abilities, for their part, arise on the basis of concrete modes of production. This assertion refers back to the general Marxian doctrine that the essential development of man is determined by the way in which he produces. Even the most barbaric or most alienated mode of production forms men in a specific way, which plays the ultimate determining role in interrelations between human groups, no matter how 'extra-economic' these may appear.

If the determination of distribution by production is considered in this way from the standpoint of the primacy of man forming and transforming himself in production, then this relationship appears immediately evident. It is only when, as was often the case within Marxism, and is still the case today, economic relations are not conceived as relationships between men, but are fetishized and 'reified'—e.g. by identifying the productive forces with a technology that is considered something autonomous and existing in itself—that this relationship becomes puzzling. Complexes of problems then arise that are difficult to resolve, such as the present industrialization of the developing countries, for instance, and which can only be resolved on the basis of this de-fetishized Marxian conception of the relation of production and distribution. Generally speaking, it is only if the position of the predominant character of production in the formation and transformation of distribution is made clearly visible, that the relation of the economic and extra-economic can be correctly understood. For our earlier assertion to the effect that the economic moment is ultimately decisive even in the extra-economic, in no way means that this difference can be treated as non-existent, as mere appearance. In our analysis of the so-called primitive accumulation, for example, we indicated that it was only when this was concluded that the genuine and purely economic laws of capitalism could become effective, which means, with reference to social being, that the new economic system of capitalism would not have been possible without this preceding extra-economic re-shuffling of the relations of distribution. Yet this is in no way an abstract and general law of development, that can be simply applied to phenomena of all kinds.

On the one hand, it is possible for even such basic alterations in the relations of distribution to take place for purely economic reasons, as was the case for example with the rise of machine industry in England, or in the USA in the last few decades. In different conditions, the same development can even assume a very different character; Lenin distinguished in the agrarian development of the capitalist era, the Prussian and the American roads; the first involved an extremely slow demolition of feudal distribution relations on the land, the second the extreme opposite, the complete absence of the radical liquidation of feudalism.[28] It is clear from this that the development of capitalism can proceed in extremely different ways according to the different tempo of this transformation.

On the other hand, however, even the directly extra-economic transformations are in the last instance economically determined; the English form of the abolition of feudal relations of distribution was directly accomplished by the most forcible means, yet this was determined by the fact that England was in transition from feudal agriculture to sheep-raising, the production of raw materials for the textile industry. Examples such as these can be multiplied endlessly. The point here, however, is not just a mere reminder to consider the facts dialectically, neither making a simple identity nor an exclusive opposition between their economic and extra-economic nature, but seeing an identity of identity and non-identity; the point is rather to take up in this case, too, the Marxian conception of reality: that the starting-point of all ideas is the actual expressions of social being. This does not mean any kind of empiricism, although, as we have seen, even this can contain an ontological *'intentio recta'*, even if half-hearted and incomplete; it is necessary, rather, to conceive every single fact as part of a dynamic complex standing in reciprocal relation with other complexes, and determined internally as well as externally by a variety of laws. The Marxian ontology of social being is based on this materialist and dialectical (contradictory) unity of law and fact (naturally including also relationships and conditions). The former is realized in the latter; and the latter obtains its concrete determination and specificity from the mode in which the former permeates it in intersecting interactions. Without understanding the way in which the real social production and reproduction of human life forms the predominant moment in these complexities, it is impossible to understand Marx's economics.

To conclude this discussion, I would like to indicate briefly how the very popular opposition of force and economics is also metaphysical and undialectical. Force, too, can be an immanent economic category. In his treatment of labour rent, for example, Marx indicated that its essence, surplus-labour, 'can only be extorted. . . by other than economic pressure.'[29] This mutual interpenetration can be traced throughout human history. From slavery, with its basis in the gradually won ability of men to produce more than was needed for their maintenance and reproduction, through to the determination of the working day under capitalism, force remains an integral moment of the economic reality of all class societies. Here, too, we see an ontological and concrete dialectic at work: The fact that they are necessarily fitted into law-like economic relationships cannot get rid of the opposition between the two, and this essential lawfulness, for its part, cannot abolish the necessity of the relationships. Once again, we see that the correct ontological conception of being must always proceed from the primary heterogeneity of the individual elements, processes and complexes, and must grasp the compulsory character of their intimate and penetrating correlation in every concrete and historical social totality. Every time that we speak of a linkage of this kind, of heterogenous and opposing complexes, we must pay attention to the concreteness of its comprehension in thought (as the reflection of its concreteness of existence), and warn against an abstract 'lawfulness' as well as of a just as abstract 'uniqueness'. At the level of our discussions so far, the demand for concreteness still remains an abstract and purely methodological postulate, and we have not yet attained the concreteness of the thing itself. The cause of this abstractness lies in the fact that up to now, in order to elaborate the most important and most general characteristics of Marx's ontology of social being, we have not given sufficient weight to one of its most decisive dimensions, the historicity of this being as a whole, in the sum of its parts, their relations towards one another, and their transformation as a result of changes in the totality and the complexes composing it—though of course we have not completely eliminated this ontological significance, which would be impossible. This lack has now to be made up, which is the task of the following section.

3. *Historicity and Theoretical Generality*

In all our ontological discussions up till now, the historicity of any social being was implicitly assumed as an existential determination, for the whole as well as in detail. We already referred to this aspect when dealing, for example, with the young Marx's conception of the universal unitary science of history—a conception that he never abandoned. Yet we believe that this half-expressed actuality of the historical is not a sufficient basis for grasping the specific ontological problems of social being; it is necessary, rather, for at least the most important categories and categorical relations to be confronted in thought which the historicity that is inherent in them.

History is an irreversible process, and it therefore seems natural to start the ontological investigation of history with the irreversibility of time. It is evident that we have here a genuine ontological relationship. If this characteristic of time were not the insuperable foundation of any existent, then the problem of the necessary historicity of being could not even arise. Certainly, the reversibility of many processes of inorganic being is not thereby abolished, which already indicates that it is impossible to get to grips with the real problem here in terms of an immediate relationship. For the irreversibility of certain physical processes can in no way be deduced simply from the abstract irreversibility of time. These processes do exist, but they can only be understood in terms of concrete material procedures and relationships; they certainly take place in time, but so do the reversible processes, and with just the same lawfulness. Even the profound partial truth of Heraclitus' saying that one can never step twice into the same river, is based on the never interrupted movement of matter, on the basic ontological fact that motion and matter form two sides and two moments of the same relationship of substantiality; the dialectical correction of this genial partial truth can only consist in seeing substantiality itself (in the form of dynamic continuity) as the basic principle. The fact that Heraclitus himself saw this relationship in no way alters this state of affairs.

It is no accident that we have brought in here the term 'substance'. For there has been a movement in philosophy ever since the beginning of the nineteenth century to eliminate substance from the view of the world. We are not so much referring to Hegel in this respect, since his tendency to transform substance into subject was ultimately aimed not at eliminating the concept of substance from philosophy, but rather of conceiving it as dynamic, historical, and bound up with the subject of the human race; even though this attempt itself was questionable enough. But this conception had no widespread and lasting effects. With neo-Kantianism and positivism, however, an epistemologically oriented dissolution of the concept of substance was proposed; Cassirer's contrast between the concepts of substance and function served here as the programme for both positivism and neo-positivism. These tendencies seemed to be based on the achievements of recent knowledge, particularly in the natural sciences, and thus contained much that was correct in their criticism of the old concepts of substance—vulgar materialism, vitalism in biology, etc. Yet they ignored the essence of the question. Substance, as the ontological principle of persistence through change, has certainly lost its old sense as an exclusive opposite to becoming, but it now acquires a new and more profound validity, in so far as persistence comes to be conceived as that which continually maintains itself, renews itself and develops in the real complexes of reality, in so far as continuity as an internal form of motion of the complex makes the abstract and static persistence into a concrete persistence within becoming. This is true even for complexes of an inorganic kind, and forms the principle of reproduction in the organism and society. This transformation of the former static concept of substance into a dynamic one, of one that degrades the world of appearance for the sake of the exclusive and single substance into the substantiality of dynamic complexes that differ so greatly among themselves, is indicated by all the new

71

achievements of science, while these also refute any kind of simple relativism, subjectivism, etc. This however has the further consequence, which is for the highest importance for our present problem, that the concept of substance ceases to stand in an exclusive antithesis to historicity, as it does most significantly with Spinoza. On the contrary, continuity in persistence, as the existential principle of dynamic complexes, demonstrates ontological tendencies towards historicity as a principle of being itself.

Yet the permanence of motion is still not sufficient to determine the specific concreteness of the historical. To put it in the most general form, the historical does not just contain a motion in general, but also and always a direction of change, a direction that is expressed in qualitative changes of specific complexes, both in themselves and in relation to other complexes. In order to demarcate what is originally and genuinely ontological here from the error put forward by the old ontology, generally described as metaphysics, a few remarks are necessary. We have already spoken in other connections of the fact that development (including development to a higher stage) has nothing to do with how this is judged in an ethical, cultural or aesthetic sense, etc. Judgements of this kind arise with ontological necessity in the context and in the course of social being, and it is a special and important task to determine their precise ontological relevance, i.e. the ontological objectivity of the values themselves. (We will begin to deal with this later on in this chapter, though in a really concrete way only in the Ethics.) These judgements—to leave out for the time being the values themselves—have nothing to do with the ontology of the historical in the general sense being discussed here, though we recognize the necessity of their social genesis, and the significance of their effect. We must also conceive direction, tempo, etc. in a very generalized sense, from a standpoint freed from immediacy. If the astronomic development that may take thousands of millions of years is excluded from the ontological realm of development, then the same error is committed as if the development of forms of life that exist for only hours or minutes is overlooked. This however is a primitive, easily overcome and essentially anthropomorphic kind of error. What is far more dangerous for the scientific comprehension of development is if the concept of development is generalized and extended, or narrowed and restricted, in an ontologically unfounded way. The expression 'ontological' must be especially stressed here. For there are important cases in which the *'intentio recta'* of everyday experience can undoubtedly indicate facts of development long before it has been possible to base these scientifically; the most significant example of this situation is certainly the phylogenetic development of species, which was known for a long time in the practice of animal or plant breeders, before any attempt was made to understand it scientifically. But as we stressed in our criticism of N. Hartmann, this *'intentio recta'* cannot be ascribed any secure direction. It is true that it may stand firmly on the ground of an immediate but indubitable reality, may be in advance of scientific knowledge, and may on occasion correct this ontologically; but precisely because this is an everyday orientation, it is frequently and necessarily permeated and distorted by everyday prejudices. The rejection of development when the tempo is too fast or too slow by the standards of immediacy has the same effect. It is still more important, however, that the most varied anthropomorphic ideas, stemming from untrustworthy generalizations from the labour process, are erected into criteria as to what really constitutes development. Especially prominent in this connection is the way that complexes of motion which, considered ontologically, have in no way a teleological character, are directly or indirectly ascribed such a character. These non-existent and merely assumed teleological projects, which are spontaneously endowed with a transcendent and religious sense, etc., are thus erected into basic principles that are supposed to decide whether a development is present and what is its ontological nature. It is not the place here to take issue with the various results of conceptions of this kind. It is sufficient to stress that our conceptions do not just reject any generalized form of teleology in inorganic and organic nature, but also in society, and confine its realm of validity to the particular acts of human social conduct of which the most significant form and model is labour.

Nevertheless, the fact of labour and its results gives rise to a completely specific structure. For although all the products of a teleological project arise and operate in terms of causality, so that their teleological genesis seems to be extinguished in their effects, they still have this characteristic which is only present in society, so that not only do they have themselves the character of a choice between alternatives, but their effects, too, in so far as they involve men, essentially generate alternatives. It is immaterial that an alternative of this kind may be quite everyday and superficial, and its immediate consequences very slight: it is still a real alternative, because it always bears within it the possibility of reacting on its subject to cause a change. What appear to be analogies in the animal world—whether a lion goes after this or that antelope, etc.—have nothing in common from an ontological point of view; for a 'choice' of this kind is purely biological, and cannot induce any kind of internal changes. The processes by which it is produced are purely epiphenomenal at the level of biological being. The social alternative, on the other hand, even when it is as deeply anchored in biology as in the case of food or sexuality, is not just confined to this realm, but always contains in it the above mentioned real possibility of a change in the choosing subject. Here, too, of course, there is a process of development, in the ontological sense, in so far as the act of the alternative also has the tendency to push back the natural boundary in the direction of sociality.

We have now arrived at a basic fact of objective development in social being. In order to draw the correct conclusions on this point as well, it is necessary to refer back time and again to the facts themselves, to their relations and structures. Individual constellations that have been discovered should in no case be uncritically taken over as the schema for others with a different arrangement. What is necessary above all is to avoid presenting the inevitability of the alternative in social practice in a voluntaristic or subjective sense. The best way to show the orientation needed is possibly by way of a brief analysis of the category of value, which is so central for Marxism. We have already seen that value, as a unity of use-value and exchange-value, assumes the establishment of socially necessary labour. And the investigation of human economic development shows quite plainly that, parallel with the development of sociality, of the pressing back of the natural boundary, the quantity of values created constantly increases at an ever rising tempo, while the labour socially necessary to their production just as constantly declines. Economically speaking, this means that the value of the individual product constantly falls as the sum of values rises. This gives a direction of development in which the increasing sociality of production is not simply expressed in an increase of products, but equally too in a decline in the labour socially necessary for their production.[1] There is no question but that this is an objective and necessary development within social being, whose ontological objectivity remains as independent of the individual acts that actually bring it about, as it does from the judgements that men make of it from the most varied standpoints and the most varied motives. We are thus confronted with an objective ontological fact of the intrinsic developmental tendency of social being.

It is an important ontological characteristic of economic value and the tendencies of its development that it is possible to establish the objectivity of a development of this kind, its complete independence of the value judgements made by men. It is necessary to stress this objectivity, although—or rather because—it does not by a long way suffice to depict the ontological phenomenon itself. Its description as 'value'—in virtually all languages—is in no way accidental. The socially real and objective relationship, independent of consciousness, that is described here by the term 'value', is, without prejudice to its objectivity, the ultimate ontological foundation—naturally only the ultimate one—for all those social relations that we refer to as values; and thus also for all those modes of behaviour of social relevance that we call value judgements. This dialectical unity of socially objective existence and objectively founded value relation is rooted in the fact that all these objective relationships, processes, etc., although they certainly maintain themselves and operate independent of the intentions of the individual human acts in which they are embodied, nevertheless only arise as the realization of these intentions, and can only develop further by way of their reaction back on further individual human acts. It is necessary to understand and maintain this duality, if the specificity of social being is to be understood: the simultaneous dependence and independence of special patterns and processes on the individual acts that directly give rise to them and perpetuate them. The many misconceptions of social being arise in great measure as a result of the fact that one of the two components is exaggerated and made into the sole or absolutely dominant one, whereas both are only real in their mutual interaction. Marx says, 'Men make their own history, but they do not make it just as they please; they do not make it under circumstances chosen by themselves, but under circumstances directly encountered, given and transmitted from the past.'[2] What Marx is particularly concerned with in this passage is the influence of tradition. It is clear, however, that the concept of 'circumstances' is understood philosophically in a very general sense. For there are no alternatives that are not concrete ones; they can never be separated from their *hic et nunc* (in the broadest sense of this expression). Yet it is precisely on account of this concreteness, which results from an inseverable collaboration between the individual man and the social circumstances of his action, that each particular alternative act receives a series of general social determinations, which—quite independently of conscious intentions—give the original act further consequences, and give rise to similarly structured new alternatives, to causal chains whose regularity necessarily goes beyond the intentions of the alternatives themselves. The objective regularity of social being is thus inseparably bound up with individual acts of an alternative character, but it also possesses a social stringency, that is independent of this.

This independence, however, is again a dialectical one. It is significantly expressed in the dialectic of appearance and essence (in which connection it must naturally be borne in mind that the materialist dialectic sees the appearance as something existent, and not as an antithesis to being). The dialectical reciprocity between the individual, the subject of the alternative, and the general, the socially lawlike, creates a more manifold and variegated series of phenomena, precisely because the social essence can only reveal its appearance via the medium of ultimately individualized man. (The specific problems that arise from this constellation will be discussed in more detail in the second part, when we go into the different relationships separately.) What we still have to indicate briefly here is a further structural problem of social being that has decisive effects on this characteristic of the relation of essence and appearance: the reflection determination between whole and part. The general ontological situation already undergoes a qualitative change in this respect between the inorganic and the organic realm; it may be questioned, and I believe not without a certain foundation, whether the organs of animals should be conceived as parts. These parts certainly possess a specification and differentiation, a life of their own which has at least a certain relative independence, such as would be impossible in the inorganic world. But since they can only exist and reproduce their relative independence in and as a consequence of their function in the total organism, they still express, at an ontologically more developed stage, the reflection relationship of the part to the whole. In social life this situation undergoes a further development. What in biological existence—at least in its immediate form—was the whole, the self-reproducing organism, becomes here a part of the social world. The increase in independence is obvious, since every man is necessarily a whole in the biological sense. The ontological problem, however, is that this very independence comes to be the bearer of the partial character in the social sense. The human individual, in so far as he is such and is not simply a biological life-form, which is never the case in reality, can just as little be separated from his concrete social totality, in the last analysis (if for other reasons and hence in a different manner), as the organ can be separated from the biological totality. The difference lies in the fact that the existence of the organ is inseparably bound up with the organism to which it belongs, while this indissoluble connection of man and society is only a function of society in general, and allows major concrete variations; the more so, the more sociality is developed. Here, too, the natural boundary retreats; for primitive man, exclusion from his society still amounts to a sentence of death. The increasing sociality of human life however arouses in many individuals the illusion of a general independence from society, a kind of existence as an isolated atom. The young Marx already protested against this conception in the case of the radical Young Hegelians.[3] And in other passages he explains these illusions of independence in terms of the 'accidental nature of the conditions of life for the individual' in capitalist society, in contrast to the situation of the estate and caste, etc., which is again in terms of the strengthening of the specific regularity of the more developed sociality and the retreat of the natural boundary.[4]

This excursus, which was necessary at this point, leads us back to a better understanding of the problem of value, in connection with the change in socially necessary labour. What is expressed in the general law of value as the quantitative decline of socially necessary labour-time in commodity production, is only one side of a total relationship, the other aspect of which is the development of the abilities of man as an individual being. In the *Grundrisse,* Marx develops this dual correlation in the following way:

'It [i.e. value, as represented by wealth: G.L.] appears in all forms in the shape of a thing, be it an object or be it a relation mediated through the object, which is external and accidental to the individual. . . In fact, however, when the limited bourgeois form is stripped away, what is wealth other than the universality of individual needs, capacities, pleasures, productive forces etc., created through universal exchange? The full development of human mastery over the forces of nature, those of so-called nature as well as of humanity's own nature? The absolute working-out of his creative potentialities, with no presupposition other than the previous historic development, which makes this totality of development, i.e. the development of all human powers as such the end in itself, not as measured on a *predetermined* yardstick? Where he does not reproduce himself in one specificity, but produces his totality? Strives not to remain something he has become, but is in the absolute movement of becoming?'[5]

It is clear that what we are dealing with here is an essentially objective development, but just as clear, too, that the fact that arises and develops here, the unfolding of human abilities and needs, forms the objective foundation for all value, and for its objectivity. It is only possible to speak of value in the context of social being; even though development in inorganic and organic being produces more developed forms, it would be mere words to describe the developed form as value. It is only in so far as the development of social being in its ontologically primary form, in the area of the economy (of labour), produces a higher development of human abilities, that its resultant, as the product of the self-activity of the human race, has a value character which is bound up with its objective existence and is inseparable from it.

If any value whatsoever is investigated for its ultimate ontological foundation, then we unfailingly come up against the development of human abilities as the orientation governing it, as its adequate object, and this as the product of human activity itself. If we ascribe to labour and its (direct and indirect) consequences for the existence of man a priority over other forms of activity in this regard, then this is purely in an ontological sense. In other words, labour is particularly from a genetic point of view the starting-point of the humanization of man, for the extension of his abilities, among which self-mastery is something that can never be forgotten. It is moreover for a very long space of time the only area of this development, and all other forms of human activity which are linked to various values can only appear in an independent form when labour itself has already reached a relatively high level. We can not investigate here how far these remain linked to labour even at a later stage; what matters here is simply this ontological priority, which, as we must ever repeat, has nothing to do with any hierarchy of values. It is simply that all values are based directly or indirectly on that which, in human terms, arises in and through labour, and precisely constitutes the realm of the human.

Our problem is not yet exhausted with this establishment

of the ontological relationship. It is no accident that in the last excursus we dealt with the relation of appearance and essence expressly in the social sense. The problem of value would be much simpler if this relation did not express itself in highly paradoxical and contradictory ways, indicating that we are dealing here with a central, extremely typical and characteristic relation within social being. Directly following the passage quoted above, Marx describes the form that this complex assumes under capitalism: 'In bourgeois economics—and in the epoch of production to which it corresponds—this complete working-out of the human content appears as a complete emptying-out, this universal objectification as total alienation, and the tearing-down of all limited, one-sided aims as sacrifice of the human end-in-itself to an entirely external end.'[6] If this relationship of essence and appearance is to be correctly understood, in its connection of value and wealth, on the one hand, and the development of human abilities on the other (both, as we have seen, form a single inseparably united complex), then it is necessary to proceed from the fact that the appearance is not only just as socially existent as the essence, but that the two are produced by the same social necessities, that they are both indissoluble components of this social and historical complex.

Within this unity, however, arise extremely important existential distinctions between the two, and these can develop into contradictions. In the law of value itself, we have the domination of a generality synthesized out of individual acts, which determines the manner, direction and tempo etc. of the social development. The individual can rebel against this only at the price of defeat, and a revolt of this kind even collapses very easily into a grotesque and quixotic caricature. This does not of course exclude revolutionary transformations, which are in their turn syntheses of innumerable individual acts; these however proceed from the whole and react on the whole. Revolutions are of course border cases, which presuppose not only the actions of masses, but also a questionable internal situation within the objective developmental tendencies. There are also important cases, however, and precisely from the standpoint of this objective sphere, in which these qualitative changes of structure and movement can give rise to a resistance, which may reach massive proportions. We need only refer to relative surplus-value, whose internal nature is far more purely social than that of absolute surplus-value, and which has developed as a result of the resistance of the working class, i.e. not simply through the internal dialectic of the internal driving force of the capitalist economy, but as a result of the class struggle. Here the ontological fact of social being that we have already stressed, that the maximum and minimum of labour-time is not determined 'purely economically', but that struggle and force are involved in deciding the concrete situation at any particular time, is expressed in a higher form.

The world of appearance described here intervenes far more directly, and more unevenly, in the personal life of individuals; the emptying-out, alienation, etc. thus in many ways more closely impinge on individual decisions, acts, etc., as the general development of human abilities proceeds, for the most part behind the backs of individuals, unconsciously in the social sense. Without going into further detail here as to this unitary and divided process, which we shall discuss later, it can already be established here that the sphere of appearance offers a far greater objective space for individual action than does that of the essence, that it is in a certain sense less impenetrable and less compulsory in its effects than the latter. This relatively relaxed character of the sphere of appearance opens up possibilities of taking up positions, modes of behaviour, etc. which in their own way—of course at times via very far-reaching, complicated and intricate mediations—can react back on the whole of social and historical occurrence.

This question, too, can only be dealt with in detail at a more concrete level. Here we can only briefly indicate a few types of these positions that are taken up in knowledge and pass over into direct behaviour; in this connection it must be stressed that although the differentiation shows a certain typology, this can have a very different character at different phases of historical development, according to the structure and tendencies of the economic formation involved. Marx's closing remarks to the two passages quoted above, which supplement one another, relate to the judgement and evaluation of the overall process in its unity of essence and appearance. He stresses here, too, the ontological priority of the overall process; Marx always theoretically opposed all romantic glorification of an undeveloped past, which played this off either economically or in a philosophy-of-history sense against objectively higher developments. But even here, where this is very decisively the case, he does not fail to refer to the contradictoriness that we have already mentioned: 'This is why the childish world of antiquity appears on one side as loftier. On the other side, it really is loftier in all matters where closed shapes, forms and given limits are sought for. It is satisfaction from a limited standpoint; while the modern gives no satisfaction; or, where it appears satisfied with itself, it is *vulgar*.'[7]

The description 'vulgar' for a satisfaction within capitalism already shows that while Marx as always sees the social and historical ontological priority of the objective principles in the overall process as central, he does not forget that the mode of appearance of this undeniable progress of the whole can stand to it—just as objectively, though at a different level—in a relationship of complete opposition, which can give rise to other judgements and behaviour that are just as objectively founded. Anyone who paid attention to our discussion of Marx's presentation of primitive accumulation will be able to follow the steps of this antithesis.

Engels gave this ontological position a clear formulation in his late Introduction to *The Poverty of Philosophy*. Speaking of the radical successors of Ricardo, who drew directly socialist conclusions from the latter's doctrine of surplus-value, Engels correctly notes that these were 'formally. . . economically incorrect'; he stresses the contrast between the moralistic arguments of the Ricardian socialists and the economic arguments of Marx. The moral problem, says Engels, 'has nothing immediately to do with economics'. At the end of his criticism, however, he writes: 'But what formally may be economically incorrect, may all the same be correct from the point of view of world history', and he points to the fact that the general moral condemnation of economic structures and tendencies may indicate their untenability even in an economic sense. 'Therefore, a very true economic content may be concealed behind the formal economic incorrectness.'[8] Engels discusses the dissolution of primitive communism in very similar terms. Here, too, he underlines first and foremost the necessity and progressiveness of this development as the primary moment from the standpoint of the ontology of social being, but adds immediately that this progress of the economic essence 'from the very start appear[ed] as a degradation, a fall from the simple moral greatness of the old gentile society. The lowest interests—base greed, brutal appetites, sordid avarice, selfish robbery of the common wealth—inaugurate the new, civilized, class society. It is by the vilest means—theft, violence, fraud, treason—that the old classless gentile society is undermined and overthrown.'[9] And history itself shows that this is not just a mere moralistic value judgement, but, just as in the cases mentioned earlier, a matter of reactions which can themselves amount to a social power. If we consider the indelible myth of the 'golden age' and trace its effect on many heretical movements right up to Rousseau and his influence on the radical Jacobins, this is again something clearly similar. This historical necessity is verified even in the purely objective change in social formations. While the dissolution of primitive communism proves itself to be the principle of economic and social progress, first in the form of slavery, then in feudalism and capitalism, the preservation of the original communities in the 'Asiatic relations of pro- duction' becomes a principle of stagnation; it should be remarked in passing that its world of appearance was in no way less characterized by the reprehensible and abominable than was the line arising in Europe. Examples could be multiplied without limit; this would be superfluous, however, since, as we hope, the most important moments of this contradictory relationship between objective development and the antithetical forms of value that necessarily arise from it have already been sufficiently illustrated. We can only discuss this problem further when we come on to speak of the question of uneven development, which was so important for Marx, and which we shall discuss in the course of our analysis of the ontological historicity of society. Everything that has been discussed here simply forms a part of this complex of questions that is of such central importance for Marxism.

The preceding considerations, despite their very introductory and incomplete character, at least indicate very important and fundamental facts: the way that forms of relationships such as development, progress, etc. are linked up with the ontological priority of complexes over their elements. History can only have the character of a complex, since the concrete components out of which it is composed, such as structure, structural change, direction, etc. are only possible within such complexes. So long as the atom was conceived of as an elementary and indivisible entity, then not only the atom itself, but also the mutual interaction of such entities, had to remain ultimately unhistorical; it is only since modern physics has discovered the atom to be a dynamic complex that it is possible to speak of genuine processes within it. The situation is similar as far as all knowledge of the inorganic world is concerned; when a kind of astronomical history emerged with the theories of Kant and Laplace, then this knowledge—no matter how far it became methodologically conscious—came to form the precondition for conceiving the solar system and its components as a complex, whose movements, changes, etc. determined the being and becoming of the 'elements', and not the other way round; it is similarly necessary to understand the earth as a complex, in order to give the knowledge that we call geology an existential foundation. In organic being this situation is still more evident; the cell could never play the same methodological role as the atom did in the inorganic world, for the reason that it is itself a complex. The birth and death of any organic being already necessarily represents a historical process on a small scale, and since Lamarck and Darwin the phylogenetic development of species has come to appear as a historical development on a grand scale. It is self-evident that history on the level of social being must develop in a still higher form, particularly to the extent that social categories come to predominate ever more over merely organic and natural ones. It is quite possible, for example, to conceive the reproduction of species from the division of cells through to the sexual life of the higher animals as a history, but it is apparent at first glance that the history of human sexuality, with its marriage, eroticism, etc. acquires an incomparable addition of richness, differentiation, gradation, creation of qualitatively new phenomena, etc. as a result of the complex of its social characteristics.

The ontological specificity of this new mode of being is expressed in this. The complex remains the general foundation of historicity, but the properties of the complex undergo a radical transformation. We should remember first of all the lability in the boundary of the complexes which is a direct result of the retreat of the natural boundary. Important as the difference in the stability of complexes between inorganic and organic nature may be, they both have the decisive common feature that they are naturally given once and for all, i.e. each complex exists with its historical development only as long as it retains its naturally given form, and its dynamic is only possible within this givenness; the birth and death of the higher organisms clearly express these restrictions to change. The complexes of social life, on the other hand, as soon as their naturalness is overcome, have a being that, while it certainly reproduces itself, yet increasingly goes beyond the simple reproduction of the originally given conditions; reproduction on an extended scale can certainly have social limits in the relations of production, but it is qualitatively different from that cessation, decline and end that is represented in the organic by old age and death. Two or more tribes can unite, one tribe can split up, etc. and the complexes that newly arise will again reproduce themselves with full value. Of course, tribes and nations can perish; but this process has nothing in common with death in organic life; even complete extermination is a social act. In the normal fashion, however, new complexes arise from splits, unifications, subjugations, etc., which further develop the new or modified processes of reproduction on the basis of their new structure and its dynamic possibilities.

An important prerequisite of this completely new situation, which we have already indicated, is that although man can only exist in society, this does not have to be (in terms of the development of being) that to which he naturally belongs by birth. Every man is certainly by nature a biological complex, and as such shares in all the specificities of organic being (birth, growth, age, death). But despite the insuperable character of this organic being, even the biological being of man has a preponderantly socially determined character, and to an increasing extent. If modern biologists, in defining the difference between man and animal, indicate, as e.g. Portmann does, the slow development of the child, his long period of helplessness and incapacity for the kind of specific independence that young animals possess soon after their birth, then they present features of this kind as biological characteristics of man. This may seem to be fairly illuminating at first glance. But it must be added that these biological properties of man are ultimately the products of society. If the species of animal from which man developed had been biologically equipped in even a similar way to that which Portmann describes, it would undoubtedly have rapidly succumbed in the struggle for existence. It is only the security, no matter how primitive and unstable, that the earliest society based on labour can offer, that can protect the new-born infants, in their slower development, even in the biological sense. A developmental tempo of this kind in the case of an animal would be quite senseless and would therefore never have arisen. It is only the major new requirements of the human being, in the process of his becoming, which derive from sociality (upright gait, speech, aptitude for labour, etc.) that make this slow development necessary, and society accordingly creates the conditions for their realization. The fact that this is only fixed biologically in the course of several tens of thousands of years, in no way alters the social character of this genesis, no more than it affects the fact that, once this biological property of man is fixed as an inherited characteristic, there can be an ever further postponement of the 'mature' condition as a result of the growing demands of social being, without specifically biological changes. A simple glance at forms of society that are even a little primitive in comparison to the present shows this tendency very clearly. It can not of course be the task of these discussions to criticize in detail problems of biology. But since the biological being of man constitutes a fundamental moment of the ontology of social being, and since pre-Marxist thought distorts the understanding and correct conception of social being by way of an impermissible 'biologization' of social categories, which are generally constructed simply by formal analogies—the list of these attempts goes from the partisan aristocratic fable of Menenius Agrippa, through to Spengler, Jung, etc. —it is necessary to give at least one example of the untenableness of such a method.

Here, already, it is shown to be a fundamental structure of social processes that they directly proceed from alternatively determined teleological projects of individual men, which however, as a consequence of the causal sequence of teleological projects, flow into a contradictory but unitary causal process of social complexes and their totality, and in general give rise to law-like relationships. The general economic tendencies that arise in this way are thus always themselves achieved syntheses of individual acts that result from the social movement itself, and henceforth acquire through this a kind of purely social and economic character, of such a kind that the majority of individual men, without needing to have a clear consciousness of this, react to the typical circumstances, constellations, chances, etc. of their time in a typically adapted way. The synthesizing resultants of movements of this kind build themselves into the objectivity of the overall process. It is a well-known fact that a relationship of this kind between individual movements and the overall process that they constitute, provides the existential foundation for what is called statistical method. In physics it has been self-evident since Boltzmann that the characteristic phenomenon is to be seen in complexes of movements of this kind, whereas it is immaterial for his classic discovery how the individual molecular movements, which Boltzmann considered as intrinsically knowable, are arranged. Their deviations from the average produce what the mathematical formulations of statistical laws call distribution; If these relationships are considered in terms of simple ontological facts, then the long reigning conception—happily represented nowadays only by a few lone wolves of mathematically fetishized neo-positivism—in which statistical laws or tendencies are placed in opposition to causality, appears a pure absurdity. The effective synthesis of typical causal series is just as causal as these are themselves, even if this unification brings to light new relationships that would otherwise be unknowable. This characteristic means that the statistical method can reveal the specific causality in the movement of complexes.

The situation depicted here, i.e. that only the typical movements of the 'elements' are involved in the knowledge of the overall process, is naturally merely a classic simple case of statistical law. We cannot go into problems of inorganic nature in any detail here. Yet it is already evident in the organic world that the interactions of general and generally relevant individual processes may present an extremely complicated picture. This is still more acute in social being, for the simple reason that man as the 'element' of economic and social relationships is himself a complex in process, whose own movements, even if of no direct practical relevance for the specific laws of economic development, may still not be a matter of indifference for the development of society as a whole. It is pertinent here, though this can only be concretely investigated in the second part, that the 'elements' of society do not just include men as specifically determined complexes, but that society is also made up of cross-cutting, coalescing and contending partial complexes such as institutions, socially determined associations of men (classes), etc., which precisely because of their different and heterogenous dimensions of existence are able to exert a decisive influence on the real interactions of the overall process. Several complications for the knowledge of the process in its totality and the interaction of its decisive moments arise from this, but these do not alter the essence of the new method, the causal relations of complexes. The complications merely have the consequence that these methods, which are comparable to the statistical in their ontological foundation, cannot in all cases be exclusively or even predominantly elaborated in terms of quantitative statistics, but frequently need to be supported, supplemented or even replaced by qualitative analyses of the real connections.

There can be no doubt that the knowledge of complex motions of this kind is generally greatly promoted by their mathematization, and it is even certain that without the mathematical expression of the quantitative and quantifiable relationships that arise here it would be scarcely possible to arrive at any exact knowledge of the laws of these complexes. Yet it does not follow from this that the ontological priority of facticity can always be mathematically homogenized at will. We have already indicated in other connections that quantity and quality are correlated reflection determinations, which has the necessary result that within certain limits (determined by the object itself) qualitative determinations cannot be quantitatively expressed without a falsification of the content. This possibility in no way means that every mathematical expression of quantitative and quantified relationships necessarily corresponds to genuine, real and important relationships. We have already had to stress in criticising the neo-positivists that every mathematically conceived phenomenon must be interpreted according to its particular ontological character, either physical or biological, etc., if the real phenomenon itself is to be understood. This requirement also holds for the statistical method; it must be even more particularly stressed here that only a mathematization that proceeds from the fixing of significant facts is able to arrive at genuine results.

Without touching here on the problem of other bordering areas, it must be pointed out that in the case of social being, and particularly in the economic realm, the subject-matter itself creates quantitative categories as a result of its own dialectic (above all those of money), and these appear directly as a given basis for mathematical and statistical treatment; however, if they are regarded in the context of the economic complex as a whole, they often lead away from the basic problems, rather than toward them. (Marx often speaks of the meaninglessness and conceptual vacuity of the pure monetary expression, when referring to such developed economic processes as reproduction, for example.) In the socialist countries, the struggle for or against a mathematical and statistical method was purely scholastic. It was ridiculous to challenge its utility in the name of a supposed Marxist orthodoxy; but it was no less foolish to imitate with uncritical enthusiasm the neopositivist vacuity. It is also relevant in this connection that Marxian economics is a criticism of political economy, and indeed, as we have shown, an ontological one. Marx's general method involves all the basic questions of principle in the internal and external laws of motion of complexes. (We need only think of the development of the average rate of profit, the laws of proportionality in accumulation, etc.) It always depends on the particular concrete question, whether and to what extent this general method should be converted into the form of directly mathematical statistics.

Important as this question may be, it is still simply one of scientific expression, and not the matter of the thing itself. This is focussed around the complex of questions about how the laws thus discovered are constituted ontologically. Bourgeois science, and particularly German science since Ranke, constructs an antithesis between law and history. History is supposed to be a process whose express uniqueness, specificity, unrepeatableness, etc. forms an antinomy to the 'external validity' of scientific laws. Because ontological questions are rejected here, this antinomy is reduced to the duality between two mutually exclusive modes of thought, and it is therefore profoundly unscientific. On the other hand, when a lawlike regularity is discovered in history, as in Spengler or in an attenuated form in Toynbee, this law is alleged to be of an eternal, 'cosmic' kind, and its cyclical character negates the continuity of history, and ultimately history itself. For Marx, however, historicity is the internal immanent law-like movement of social being itself. (We have already drawn attention to the general questions of the historicity of all dynamic complexes at the various levels of being.) Historically, social being arises out of the inorganic and organic world, and it is ontologically impossible for it to leave this basis behind. The central means of mediation which thus rises more and more energetically above mere naturalness, and is yet rooted in it in an insuperable way, is labour: 'So far therefore as labour is a creator of use-value, is useful labour, it is a necessary condition, independent of all forms of society, for the existence of the human race; it is an eternal nature-imposed necessity, without which there can be no material exchanges between man and Nature, and therefore no life.'[10] In this way there arises the only objective and quite general law of social being, which is as 'eternal' as social being itself, and is also a historical law, in so far as it arises simultaneously with social being, and remains effective just as long as this exists. All other laws that are situated within social being are thus already of a historical character. Marx demonstrated the genesis of the most general of these, the law of value, in the introductory chapter of his master-work. This is indeed immanent to labour itself, in so far as it is linked by labour-time with labour itself as the development of human abilities and is already implicitly present when man has only reached the stage of useful labour, when his products have not yet become values; it remains just as implicitly valid after the sale and purchase of commodities have come to an end.[11] The law of value only acquires its developed and explicit form, however, when the reflection relation of use-value and exchange-value comes into being, and exchange-value acquires its specific and purely social form, independent of any natural characteristic. All other laws of economics are of a purely historical character, without prejudice to their lawfulness, which in fact has a tendential character as law of dynamic complexes; this means that they acquire and retain their validity depending on specific social and historical circumstances, whose presence or absence is not, or at least not directly produced by the law itself. It is part of the ontological nature of the laws governing complexes, that when they come into operation, the heterogeneity of relations, forces, tendencies, etc. that compose the complexes themselves, and that stand in a reciprocal relation both to the internal constitution of the complex and to its external efficacy, must find its expression. This is why the majority of economic laws possess a validity that is concretely circumscribed, in a social and historical sense, is historically specific. Ontologically considered, law and historicity are not opposites but rather closely intertwined forms of expression of a reality which is essentially composed of various heterogenous and heterogenously moving complexes, and combines these into a unity in characteristic and equally specific laws.

If we consider the laws of social being elaborated by Marx from this ontological point of view, which is the only adequate one, then all prejudices of a mechanical and fatalistic form of law, an over-stretched and one-sided rationalism in his world view, must simply be abandoned. Marx himself consistently applied this perspective on reality in his own method. He continuously regarded this approach as theoretically correct, even if, as in many other questions, he never came round to systematically setting down his opinion in a conclusive form. In the important *Introduction* from the 1850s, which remained incomplete, and which we have already discussed in detail in considering Marx's methodological views, he wrote in the final section, which remained a mere sketch: *'This conception appears as necessary development.* But legitimation of chance.'[12] Even this role of chance within the necessity of the laws, is only something unitary, from the viewpoint of logic and epistemology, in so far as chance—certainly in different ways in different systems—is conceived as an ideal and ultimately also a supplementary antithesis to necessity. Viewed ontologically, chance, corresponding to the heterogeneity of reality, emerges in extremely different ways; as deviation from the average, as distribution in statistical laws, as the heterogenous and chance relationship of two complexes and their laws, etc. Relevant here, as the particular characteristic of social being, is the alternative character of the individual teleological projects that are directly at its basis. For a manifold role of chance is present here in an indelible way.

Let us take up again the case of labour, which is both the most central and the relatively simplest. The very fact that its foundation is the metabolism between man (society) and nature reveals an insuperable accidental character. No natural object can contain in it as one of its properties, its own laws, any kind of orientation to its suitability (or unsuitability) for human purposes, as a means of labour, raw material, etc. It is naturally the indispensable condition of any teleological project in labour that these properties and laws of the object are suitably known. Yet the chance character in the relationship of the stone to the statue or the wood to the table is not thereby abolished; stone and wood are brought into relationships that not only do not occur in their natural being, but could not occur, and which must therefore always remain accidental from the standpoint of their natural givenness, even though—we repeat—knowledge of their relevant properties constitutes the indispensable precondition for successful labour. It is interesting to see how this relationship is precisely expressed in everyday speech: when a natural material as such constitutes the foundation of an aesthetic elaboration, as in the plastic arts, architecture or handicrafts etc., there is a very particular sense in which we speak of the product being authentic to the material *[materialecht]*, for even in an otherwise technically perfect achievement, the product being true to the material *[materialecht]*, for medium is of a purely social character, of course, as in speech, and the tonal system of music, this question does not arise. This manifold relationship between labour and its natural foundation becomes still more intense as a result of the fact that labour, i.e. its technique, is determined by the capacities and knowledge of men on which it is based, i.e. purely socially. The development of labour embodies the effects of these two factors. Even the most fundamental steps forwards, the most important technical innovations and the scientific foundations for these, which always emerge later, are very often hit upon by accident; they very often appear simultaneously in different places, independently of one another. The components of social necessity certainly form the predominant moment; yet there is still an element of chance in the natural connection. It is relevant here that the alternative, as characteristic of any act of labour, also contains an element of chance.

It is also not difficult to see that, the more developed a society is, the broader and more ramified are the mediations that link the teleological project of labour with its actual accomplishment, and the role of chance must correspondingly increase. The chance relationship between natural material and its socially determined working-up often fades, and even seems to disappear in very far-reaching mediations—for example in the legal system as a moment of mediation—yet the element of chance still increases in the individual alternatives; and this is all the more so, the more ramified these become, the more removed they are from labour itself, and the more their content is oriented to inducing men to a further mediation by way of a mediating act. The concrete problems that arise in this connection can only be dealt with in the analysis of labour itself. What must be added here is simply that as far as the forces of mediation that have necessarily arisen historically in society (institutions, ideologies, etc.), are concerned, the more developed these become, and the more they are accordingly perfected in an immanent sense, the more they then acquire an internal independence, which is continuously at work in practice and leads to an increase in the quantity and quality of the chance connections—without prejudice to the ultimate dependence of these on economic laws.[13] This rough sketch can indicate only very incompletely the broad space for chance in the operation of the general and objective laws of economics, particularly because this space encompasses numerous areas of economic development.

All this has still not brought us to the central question. If we want now to deal briefly with the class struggle, then we must confine ourselves to our present problem. Because the class struggle in social practice is always a synthesis of economic law and extra-economic components of the same social reality, it is exclusively a question here of whether and to what extent moments of chance intervene in the functioning of economic laws. We have already indicated in several places that the space for extra-economic forces is created and invested by the economy itself. (Determination of labour-time by struggle, relative surplus-value as product of the class struggle, primitive accumulation, specific forms of distribution, etc.) What this involves above all, as far as the interaction of the economy and extra-economic force is concerned, are two things. Firstly, the economic laws eventually work themselves out, even if by detours that are perhaps caused by an unsatisfactory outcome of the action of classes; the succession and progression of economic formations, and the possible forms of class struggle that result from this are strongly determined in their broad and fundamental tendencies by the general laws of the economy. Secondly, however, this determinacy can not adequately extend to particulars, to the individual conflicts that arise. The major and multiform space of accident that we have sketched out does not only influence the decision of individual alternatives and collisions, but it has a far more important role in the overall process, in so far as the operation of general economic laws can take place in very different and even opposing ways, without their basic character being altered; these ways can then react back on the class struggle, which is in turn not without influence on the manner in which the general economic laws are realized, etc. etc. We need only think of how the rise of capitalism in England and France had quite different effects on agrarian relations in the two countries; this led to the bourgeois revolution taking place in quite different forms, which in turn contributed to the development of different structural forms in the capitalism of the two countries.[14]

The ontological analysis thus gives rise to a situation that appears paradoxical for logic and epistemology, and which, so long as we investigate it simply on the basis of these disciplines, can lead and has led to apparently unsolvable antinomies; ontologically considered, however, these given forms of interactions and reciprocities in social being can be understood very simply. The difficulty arises from the logical and epistemological conception of law and rationality. Seen ontologically, law simply means that within an existent complex, or in the reciprocal connection of two or several such complexes, the actual presence of definite conditions necessarily carries with it definite consequences, at least tendentially. If man succeeds in observing a relationship of this kind, and fixing in thought the circumstances under which it is necessarily repeated, then it is called rational. If many relationships of this kind are established, as already happened relatively early on, then a conceptual apparatus gradually arises in order to comprehend them and express them as exactly as possible. It cannot be our task here to discuss this development, even just by way of indicating it. It must be noted, however, that the more exactly this conceptual apparatus is constructed—particularly in the case of mathematics, geometry and logic—and the more success-fully it functions in many individual cases, the stronger grows the inclination to ascribe it, with the aid of extrapolations, a general significance that is independent of the facts of the real world, and even lays down the law to them. (It should not be forgotten that the generalized application of magical rites, formulae, etc. to whole different groups of phenomena because of analogies in their conceptual structure, already displays a certain similarity to this extrapolation.) This gives rise to the attempt, that is never completely successful, to comprehend the whole of reality, nature as well as society, as a unitary and rational connection, and to ascribe the inability to practically fulfil this attempt simply to the incomplete-ness of present knowledge.

A logical and epistemological conception of the laws governing factual relations and processes gives rise to a view of the world that is sometimes described as rationalist, and which has been expressed in different epochs in numerous important and influential philosophies. Whatever the form in which such an all-embracing rationality is formulated, it contradicts the ontological basis of all being which we have sought to elaborate: the heterogenous structure of the real world, which leads not only to the ultimately insuperable element of chance in the interactions of moments within a complex and the interactions of complexes with one another, but also to the insuperable relation between facts which are simply given (which often, as in the case of constants, cannot be rationalized any further), and the concrete rationality of definite connections that arises from these relationships. We have also pointed out this kind of existential property must constantly increase with the increasing complication of levels of existence. What we have not mentioned in this connection is a problem that is most important in the history of philosophy, the link between the rationality of being and the meaning or meaninglessness of human life, since it will only be possible to discuss this adequately in the context of our Ethics. We would simply remark here that this question can only be consistently posed if one proceeds from the complete ontological neutrality of any kind of natural being in relation to the problem of meaning. This question is far more complicated in the case of social life; although the laws of being in this sphere are still completely neutral in their objective ontological character in relation to the problem of meaningful life, yet in so far as they are inseparably linked in their objective development with the development of human capacities, as we have already shown, important reciprocities arise here which go far beyond direct social behaviour, and which can also only be treated concretely in the Ethics. Any departure from this leads to distortions and errors. This reference to a problem that is provisionally left aside may be more satisfactory in so far as even though a genuine ethics must in any case recognize the ontological neutrality of the laws of social being in its generality, it can only find and elucidate its own categories on the basis of the complicated double perspective on social being which we indicated in our analysis of the law of value.

A further important moment of the logical and epistemological over-extension that affects this question is the attempt to link up the rationality that is recognized here with calculability: *'savoir pour prévoir'* as the criterion of a rationally adequate knowledge of the world. Astronomy of course provided the original model for this; but even in inorganic nature there are complexes, such as the unpredictability of the weather, for example, that are very problematic in this respect, and if today it is possible to relate this to a considerable extent to the lack of exact foundations and sufficient observations, a doubt still remains as to whether it will ever be possible to reach the same exactness of prediction as in the case of astronomy. In biology, and especially in medicine as applied biology, the organism, as a far more concrete and existentially determining individual, provides a space for unforeseeable accidents. If we take account, here too, of the future possibility of overcoming present obstacles, we are still faced with the great qualitative complexity of social life that has been depicted, and which is what concerns us here. This does not of course rule out a short-term predictability in particular concrete cases on a restricted terrain; every act of labour and every social practice rests on this possibility, and the neopositivist theory of manipulation, which confines itself to this and rules out all ontological questions, imagines it has thereby attained a scientifically founded rationalism. We have already criticized this conception, and in dealing with labour we shall come on to speak of it again.* What we are concerned with at this point is the general rationality of scientific laws, and how constraining and concrete implications can be drawn from these for individual cases, how social being in its totality and in detail can be erected into a closed rational system. The representatives of the Enlightenment and their successors were full of ideas of this kind, and the irrationalist reaction that followed the French Revolution particularly attacked this. This led to the opposite and much falser extreme, for irrationalism completely lacks any ontological foundation. We already saw how its opponents went beyond ontological reality with logical and epistemological extrapolations, but irrationalism is no longer an extrapolation—it is no more than a subjective projection of a purely ideal discouragement in the face of a real question, which is given the deceptive form of an irrational response as a result of its irresolvability for the subject.

The extremely significant fact of rationality shows *post festum,* in the case of science, and social science in particular, to what extent both the metaphysically extrapolating universalistic rationalism and its antipode, all forms of irrationalism, move in the magic circle of an unreal antinomy. The practice of every historical science has always operated spontaneously with a method of this kind. The point here, however, is not simply to establish this fact, but first and foremost to demonstrate the existential property that gives it its ontological foundation. Any irrationalist interpretation reveals its total nullity in this connection: for it is an essential characteristic of behaviour, both individual and that of social groups, to have to make decisions in circumstances that are not, or are not completely understood, and to carry out corresponding actions. In both cases, it can subsequently be shown—and it makes no difference whether this 'subsequently' is a matter of days or centuries—that an event that originally appeared as incomprehensible, or even as completely meaningless, was entirely located in the necessary causal progression of history, in the subsequent light of the knowledge of the interaction of causes that brought it about. The rationality that arises in this way must naturally differ greatly from the axiomatics of philosophical rationalism, in so far as the accomplishment of laws follows very intricate paths, and these exhibit the large-scale role of chance. But since the existential connection between the laws and the actual facts (real complexes and their real relationships) becomes comprehensible, the rationality that is inherent to the real events becomes visible. This departure from rationalist ideas and the expectations linked to them is naturally independent of whether these expectations are disappointed or fulfilled: what is involved is the genuine validation of the objectivity of social being. Lenin gives a clear depiction of this situation in speaking of revolutions: 'History as a whole, and the history of revolutions in particular, is always richer in content, more varied, more multiform, more lively and ingenious than is imagined by even the best parties, the most class-conscious vanguards of the most advanced classes.'[15] This 'ingenuity' in the progress of events is what human behaviour has to orient itself to; it has a reasonable and law-like, i.e. rational aspect to it, but it is structured quite differently from how philosophical rationalism assumes.

This brings us back to our starting-point. For Marx, dialectical knowledge has a merely approximate character, and this is because reality consists of the incessant interaction of complexes, which are located both internally and externally in heterogenous relationships, and are themselves dynamic syntheses of often heterogenous components, so that the number of effective elements can be quite unlimited. This approximate character of knowledge is therefore not primarily something epistemological, though it of course also affects epistemology; it is rather the reflection in knowledge of the ontological determinacy of being itself: the infinity and heterogeneity of the objectively operative factors and the major consequences of this situation, i.e. that scientific laws can only fulfil themselves in the real world as tendencies, and necessities only in the tangle of opposing forces, only in a mediation that takes place by way of endless accidents. This structure of social being in no way means that it is un-knowable, or even that the possibility of knowing it is reduced. As we have already shown, it has proved completely possible to discover the most general laws of motion of the economy, and with their aid, the general line of historical development, not merely contingently, but conceptually. We have already established this definite and precise knowledge of law in connection with the problem of value. It is in no way weakened, but rather strengthened still further, if social being is considered in its historical movement. Knowledge of the development of earlier social formations, of the transition from one to the other, is naturally a *post festum* knowledge. This, too, is related to the qualitative changes that social being undergoes. A science of economics (and its internal criticism) could only arise after purely social categories had become the 'forms of being, characteristics of existence' that were dominant in social life, i.e. after the interrelation of the pre-dominantly purely economic relationships that rule its direction of movement and its tempo, etc. had become known. It was only this situation that brought about the possibility of establishing general laws of economics (something that a genius such as Aristotle, despite his penetrating insight into certain important questions, was unable to tackle.) This is of course only in general forms. When Marx investigated the conditions for economic crisis, for example, he confined him-self to an extremely general structural analysis: 'The possibility of a crisis, in so far as it shows itself in the simple form of a metamorphosis, thus only arises from the fact that the differences in form—the phases—which it passes through in the course of its progress, are in the first place necessarily complementary and secondly, despite this intrinsic and necessary correlation, they are distinct parts and forms of the process, independent of each other, diverging in time and space, separable and separated from each other.' It follows from this that the crisis is 'nothing but the forcible assertion of the unity of phases of the production process which have become independent of each other.'[16] This establishes a decisive characteristic of the crisis; it would be a foolish illusion, however, to believe that it would henceforth be possible to predict the time of outbreak of individual crises, in the way that Newtonian astronomy made it possible to predict the movements of the planets. (The fact that the character of economic crises has since changed in many ways, and that defence measures have been taken against them, possibly successfully, in no way changes this methodological situation. It simply presents Marxists who have liberated themselves from Stalinism with the task of suitably analysing the new phenomenon using the Marxian method.)

Marx's distinction between essence and appearance within the sphere of being, which we have already described, makes it possible to grasp conceptually the extremely complicated and heterogenous phenomena of the real world, including, in certain circumstances, those in the realm of individual life and its practice. There is certainly the danger in the path from the general to the particular of overestimating the direct validity of general laws in a mechanical fashion, and falsifying the facts by too direct an application; on the path from the particular to the general, on the other hand, there arises the opposite danger of a practicism devoid of ideas, and a blindness towards the degree to which even the everyday life of individual men is itself the product of the direct and indirect operation of general laws. We have already indicated in our general characterization of Marx's method that, in the programmatic formulation of his basic perspective as a 'Critique of Political Economy', it is the permanent and constantly repeated ontological criticism of the facts and their connections and laws, together with the concrete application of these, which forms at least one decisive methodological principle. This holds, too, for the paths of knowledge dealt with here, from the general to the particular and from the particular to the general. It is not sufficient to have a general insight into the structure of social being as explained above, which is what determines these paths, their direction and ramifications, etc. Just as Marx held abstractions and generalizations to be indispensable for the process of knowledge, as we have already seen, so the specification of concrete complexes and relationships seemed to him equally indispensable. Specification should be understood here in an ontological sense: the investigation of the way that particular laws, their concrete expression, variation, tendential form and their particular mode of operation, affect specific concrete complexes in specific concrete circumstances. Knowledge can only find its way to objects of this kind by investigating the particular features of any objective complex. This is why Marx says with reference to the knowledge of a complex of such central importance as uneven development: 'The difficulty consists only in the general formulation of these contradictions. As soon as they have been specified, they are already clarified.'[17] The significance of this statement goes far beyond this particular occasion, even though, as we shall see, it is certainly no accident that it is put forward in the discussion of uneven development. What is expressed here is in fact the duality of viewpoints, which must nevertheless form a unity, that is so characteristic of the Marxian ontology of social being: the unity of general law and particular developmental tendency which are separable analytically in thought, but indissoluble ontologically. The ontological correlation of heterogenous processes within a complex, or in the relations between several complexes, is what forms the existential basis for their—ever conditional—analytical separation. Ontologically, the question is one of grasping the precise nature of a complex of phenomena in relation to the general laws that condition it and from which it simultaneously appears to deviate.

This method thus seems to represent a *tertium datur* in relation to the antinomy of rationalism and empiricism which is so time-worn in the history of philosophy. Orientation to the facticity of being, as the synthesis of heterogenous moments, suspends the fetishizing involved in a rationalism and empiricism that are predominantly epistemologically oriented. We have already spoken of the fetishizing of reason; this also gives rise to the danger, for an adequate understanding of historicity, of reducing the historical process far too directly to the concept (to a concept that is abstractly distorted), and hence not only ignoring the failing to consider phases and steps that are important for the facticity, but also ascribing the overall process an over-determined rectilinearity, by over-rationalizing it, which can lead to giving it a fatalistic and even teleological character. The epistemologically rooted empiricist fetishization leads to what Hegel wittily described as the 'customary tenderness for things',[18] which means that their deeper contradictions and their connection with fundamental laws are obliterated, and the facticity devolves on this objectifying and rigidifying fetishization, which always arises when the results of a process are considered only in their ultimate and finished form, and not also in their real and contradictory genesis. Reality is fetishized into an immediate and vacuous 'uniqueness' or 'singularity', which can thus easily be built up into an irrationalist myth. In both cases, such fundamental ontological category relations as that of appearance and essence and that of individuality, particularity and generality are ignored and the image of the real world is thus endowed with a distorting and immoderate homogeneity. It is striking, though not surprising, that most of the deviations from Marxism follow one of these paths in their methods, and revoke Marx's supersession of a false antinomy in a bourgeois sense. Although we cannot go into this question in more detail here, it should be noted that sectarian dogmatism generally takes the path of a fetishization of reason, whereas opportunist revisions of Marxism commonly show the tendency to an empiricist fetishization. (There are naturally the most diverse forms of mixtures.)

This ontological inseparability of historicity and genuine rational law in the overall process, for Marxism, is all too frequently—one could even say regularly—misunderstood. Hegel gave the philosophic rationalist conception of progress its most fascinating expression, and it was very simple to carry this over into Marxism—turning it upside down in a materialist sense and giving proper predominance to the economic—and thus making a new kind of philosophy of history. Marx himself always protested against such interpretations of his method. The clearest example of this is in a letter (late 1877) to the editors of the Russian magazine *Otetchestvenniye Zapiski,* protesting against an impermissible philosophical generalization of his theory of primitive accumulation, as if the form this took in western Europe was an unchangeable law, which would necessarily apply in advance to Russia as well. Marx did not deny that he had established a law in the course of economic development, but this was simply in the form of a tendency that necessarily took shape in certain specific conditions. 'That is all. But that is too little for my critic. He feels he absolutely must metamorphose my historical sketch of the genesis of capitalism in Western Europe into a historico-philosophic theory of the general path every people is fated to tread, whatever the historical circumstances in which it finds itself, in order that it may ultimately arrive at the form of economy which ensures, together with the greatest expansion of the productive powers of social labour, the most complete development of man. But I beg his pardon. (He is both honouring and shaming me too much.)'[19]

Marx's protest against a 'historico-philosophic' generalization of his historical method is very closely connected with the criticism of Hegel of his youth. We have already observed how Marx always objected to Hegel's transformation of real relationships in the real world into logically necessary conclusions of thought. This is naturally first and foremost a criticism of Hegel's philosophical idealism, but it is also a criticism of the logical foundations of the philosophy of history (something that can be separated neither from its own specificity nor from Marx's criticism). In Hegel, the succession of historical epochs and the patterns in them (most clearly in the history of philosophy) correspond by methodological necessity to the derivation of logical categories. In Marx, however, these categories are never embodiments of mind on the path from substance to subject, but simply 'forms of being, characteristics of existence', which must be understood ontologically, just as they are, within the complexes in which they exist and become operative. It is an important method-ological means towards their knowledge that the processes as a result of which the categories arise, exist, and disappear have their law-like rationality and hence their own logic, but this is not the real foundation of their being, as it is in Hegel. If this methodologically decisive criticism of Hegel is neglected, and this construction on the basis of logic is maintained—despite a materialist reversal of all the external signs—then Marxism is left with a Hegelian systematicity that is not overcome, and the ontological and critical historicity of the overall process appears as a logical philosophy of history in the Hegelian sense.

There is no need to give a list of examples in order to show that the interpretation of Marxism is full of this kind of residue from the Hegelian philosophy of history, culminating on occasion, despite all materialism, in a logically mediated teleological necessity of socialism. It would scarcely be necessary to combat these ideas, after what has already been said and explained, were it not for the fact that Engels him-self occasionally succumbed to the fascination with Hegel's logicization of history. In one of his reviews of Marx's *A Contribution to the Critique of Political Economy* Engels puts forward the methodological dilemma of 'historical or logical', and decides: 'The logical method of treatment was, therefore, the only appropriate one. But this, as a matter of fact, is nothing else but the historical method, only divested of its historical form and disturbing fortuities. The chain of thought must begin with the same thing with which this history begins, and its further course will be nothing else but the reflection of the historical course in abstract and theoretically consistent form; a corrected reflection but corrected according to laws furnished by the real course of history itself, in that each factor can be considered at the point of development of its full maturity, of its classic form.'[20] Since we are going on straightaway to consider the Marxian conception of classicism in detail, a criticism of Engels' concluding remark is unnecessary here—a remark in which Engels conceives these categories that are only applicable to total complexes as the property of individual moments, in contrast to his own later conception, which we shall also come on to speak of in detail in its proper place. The decisive contrast with Marx's conception lies in the primacy given to the 'logical method of treatment', which is said here to be identical with the historical method, 'only divested of its historical form and disturbing fortuities'. History divested of the historical form—this is the essence of Engels' retreat to Hegel. In Hegel's philosophy this was possible; since history and the whole of reality simply appeared as a realization of logic, the system could liberate historical event from its historical form and refer it back to its proper being, i.e. to logic. But for Marx, and generally for Engels, too, historicity is an ontological property of the movement of matter which is not further reducible, and this is particularly significant when, as is the case here, it is exclusively social being that is under discussion. It is possible to grasp the most general laws of this being in a logical sense, but it is not possible to ascribe or reduce them to logic. Engels' expression 'disturbing fortuities' shows that this is what is being done here; but ontologically, it is quite possible for something accidental to be the bearer of an essential tendency, irrespective of whether this accident is conceived as 'disturbing' from the purely logical standpoint.

It is not our task here to criticize Engels' conception in any detail. It was simply necessary to indicate briefly its opposition to that of Marx. Marx always proceeds, and particularly in the Introduction to the *Grundrisse,* from the starting-point that the historical position of individual

categories can only be understood in their historical concreteness, in the historical specificity that the existing social
formation ascribes to them, and never simply in terms of
their logical characteristics, e.g. whether simple or developed.
Marx stresses that 'the simple categories are the expressions
of relations within which the less developed concrete may
have already realized itself before having posited the more
many-sided connection or relation which is mentally expressed
in the more concrete category; while the more developed
concrete preserves the same category as a subordinate
relation'.[21] This is the case with money, for example. 'To
that extent the path of abstract thought, rising from the
simple to the combined, would correspond to the real
historical process.' Marx immediately indicates, however,
that there can be very undeveloped forms of economy in
which 'highest forms of economy, e.g. cooperation, a
developed division of labour, etc. are found', even though
there is no kind of money, as e.g. in Peru.[22] As far as such a
central category as labour is concerned, 'Labour seems a quite
simple category. The conception of labour in this general
form—as labour as such—is also immeasurably old. Nevertheless, when it is economically conceived in this simplicity,
"labour" is as modern a category as are the relations which
create this simple abstraction.'[23]

Several examples could easily be given from this very rich
text, but we will confine ourselves here to the methodological
conclusion: 'Bourgeois society is the most developed and the
most complex historic organization of production. The
categories which express its relations, the comprehension of
its structure, thereby also allow insights into the structure and
the relations of production of all the vanished social formations out of whose ruins and elements it built itself up, whose
partly still unconquered remnants are carried along within it,
whose mere nuances have developed explicit significance
within it, etc. Human anatomy contains a key to the anatomy

of the ape. The imitations of higher development among the subordinate animal species, however, can be understood only after the higher development is already known. The bourgeois economy thus supplies the key to the ancient, etc.'[24] We thus find here a confirmation of earlier indications, i.e. the ontological necessity of the major tendencies of the overall development which prescribe a *post festum* knowledge.

Two things follow from this. On the one hand, this necessity is certainly to be understood rationally, even if only *post festum,* which means that any rationalist over-extension into a purely logical necessity must be strictly rejected. While it is true that classical antiquity arose with an existential necessity, and was just as necessarily replaced by feudalism, etc. it cannot be said that serfdom 'follows' from slavery in any rational or logical sense. It is of course possible to draw conclusions from *post festum* analyses and facts that are applicable to analogous development, just as general future tendencies can be deduced from knowledge of earlier general ones. But this ontological necessity is immediately falsified if the attempt is made to derive a logically based 'philosophy of history' from it. On the other hand, this existential structure is only ontologically possible in the concrete dynamic complexes that constitute (relative) totalities. 'Elements' (i.e. individual categories) that are taken by themselves, outside the wholes in which they have their real existence, have no proper historicity. In so far as these are partial totalities, complexes that move relatively independently according to their own laws, then the process of their being is also historical. Thus for example the life of a single man, or the existence of those patterns, complexes, etc. that arise within a society as relatively independent forms of being, such as the development of a class, etc. But since the self-movement that is operative here can only have its effect in interaction with the complex to which it belongs, this independence is relative and takes extremely different forms in different structural and historical circumstances. We shall deal with the dialectic of this situation further in connection with uneven development. For the moment, these remarks must suffice.

What we have to do now is to present the relation between the general regularity of the economy and the overall process of social and historical development in a few especially significant cases. One case that is significant in this way is what Marx calls the 'classicism' of a phase of development. The most significant example of this is his definition of the development of capitalism in England as a classical one. In this connection, Marx clearly explains what this definition means methodologically. He refers to the physicist who studies natural processes where these 'occur in their most typical form and most free from disturbing influence': this idea is consistently extended to stress the importance of experiment, which helps to achieve conditions 'that assure the occurrence of the phenomenon in its normality.' Now it is clear to anyone that it is an essential feature of social being that experiments in the sense of the natural sciences are in general ontologically impossible as a result of the specific predominance of the historical as the foundation and form of motion of this being itself. If the functioning of general economic laws is to be investigated in the real world itself in as pure a form as possible, then it is necessary to find steps of historical development in which particularly favourable circumstances create configurations of social complexes and their relationships in which these general laws obtain a high degree of development, undisturbed by foreign components. It is from such considerations that Marx says: 'Up to the present time, their classic ground is England' (i.e. the ground of capitalist relations).[25] The restriction 'up to the present time' needs to be particularly stressed here. This refers to the fact that the classicism of a phase of economic development is a purely historical characteristic. It is by chance that the heterogenous components of the social edifice and its development produce such and such circumstances and conditions. If we use here the phrase 'by chance', we must once again recall the ontological, objective and strongly causal and determined character of this category. Since its efficacy refers above all to the heterogenous property of the relations of social complexes, it is only *post festum* that it is possible to establish the strong character of its validity, and to understand it as necessary and rational. And because the weight, impetus, proportions, etc, of heterogenous complexes undergo continuous changes in this interaction, the causal reciprocities that arise in this manner can in certain circumstances lead away from classicism in the same way that they led towards it. The historical character of constellations of this kind is therefore expressed above all in the fact that the classicism in no way represents an 'eternal' type, but is rather the purest possible mode of appearance of a specific formation, or possibly even of one of its particular phases. Marx's definition of the past and present of English development as classical thus in no way excludes the possibility that we may be justified today in considering the American form as classical.

Engels' analysis of a much earlier and more primitive formation, the rise and development of the ancient *polis,* illustrates this situation very well in a still more concrete form. He considers Athens as the classical expression of this formation: 'Athens provides the purest, classic form; here the state springs directly and mainly out of the class oppositions which develop within gentile society itself.' In another passage he depicts this form of development as follows: 'The rise of the state among the Athenians is a particularly typical example of the formation of a state; first, the process takes place in a pure form without any interference through use of violent force either from without or from within. . .; second, it shows a very highly developed form of state, the democratic

114

republic, arising directly out of gentile society.'[26] Corresponding to the nature of this undeveloped formation, Engels places the accent on the fact that the Athenian state arose out of the interactions of internal social forces, and not, as most others of this time, as a result of external conquest and subjugation. He also stresses that at this stage, the purely social immanence in the working-out of the given economic and social forces was still completely the result of accidental and fortuitous individual cases. From the standpoint of the economic structure, the economic developmental tendencies and possibilities, the question here is one which we have already discussed in its general aspects, i.e. one of the relation between production and distribution in that broad and general sense in which it was used by Marx. The classical development thus depends on whether the productive forces of a particular region and a particular stage possess the internal power to arrange the relations of distribution after their own fashion, or whether external and predominantly extra-economic violence has to be employed in order to achieve the condition that has become economically necessary. It is evident that in the case of the Greek city state which Engels discusses, foreign conquest was the most frequent case of a non-classical development of this kind. Naturally, a development of the kind that depends on the mobilization of purely internal forces in no way rules out the use of violence, and Engels himself speaks of the importance of class struggles in the classical development of Athens. There is however a qualitative difference, depending on whether violence is one moment, the organ by which a development governed by internal economic forces is accomplished, or whether it creates completely new conditions for the economy by way of a direct reshuffling of the distribution relations. It is significant that when Marx, in *Capital,* describes the capitalist development in England as 'classical', he does not begin with the forcible rise of this development by way of primitive accumulation, the forcible reshuffling of the relations of distribution and the production of the 'free' worker indispensable for capitalism, but it is only after he has comprehensively presented the economic laws in their classical expression that he comes on to speak of this real genesis, and he does not forget to note here that: 'In the ordinary run of things, the labourer can be left to the "natural laws of production", i.e. to his dependence on capital, a dependence springing from, and guaranteed in perpetuity by, the conditions of production themselves. It is otherwise during the historical genesis of capitalist production.'[27] Thus England only became the classical country of capitalism after and as a result of this primitive accumulation.

If we are to understand correctly Marx's concept of classical development, we must insist, on this question, too, on its completely value-free and objective character. What Marx calls 'classical' is simply a development in which the economic forces that are ultimately determinant find an expression that is clearer, more perceptible, less disturbed and refracted than elsewhere. It would never be possible to directly 'derive' a superiority to other types of *polis* simply from the classicism of the Athenian development, the less so, in that this was something present only in particular regions at a particular time. Social patterns that have not arisen in classical form can be just as viable as classical ones, and even more so in many respects. Thus the opposition of classical and non-classical does not have a very great value as a measure of such viability. It has a greater value for knowledge, however, as a 'model' already present in the real world itself of the relatively pure operation of economic law. Marx says of the nature and limits of this kind of knowledge: 'One nation can and should learn from others. And even when a society has got upon the right track for the discovery of the natural laws of its movement—and it is the ultimate aim of this work, to lay bare the economic law of motion of modern society—it can neither clear by bold steps, nor remove by legal enactments, the obstacles offered by the successive phases of its normal development. But it can shorten and lessen the birth-pangs.'[28] This suggestion of Marx's, which is extremely seldom esteemed at its true value, has a major practical significance, and when it is correctly followed up, the specificity of the classical precisely plays an important role. We can take such a strongly contested question as the development of socialism in the Soviet Union. There can be no doubt today that this has repeatedly proved its viability in the most diverse fields. But it is just as certain that it was not the product of a classical development. If Marx held in his time that the socialist revolution would triumph first in the developed capitalist countries, he was thinking once again of the connection between production and distribution which we have explained here. The transition to socialism can undoubtedly involve important reshuffling in this respect, too; in the highly developed capitalist countries, however, the distribution of the population already corresponds to the requirements of an achieved social production, whereas backward countries can only stand at the beginning or in the middle of this process. Lenin realized quite clearly, in accordance with this knowledge, that the socialist revolution in Russia could not have a classical character. When he spoke of the international significance of the Russian revolution in his book *'Left-Wing' Communism: An Infantile Disorder,* he stressed this point unmistakeably, even while emphasizing the international importance of the fact itself and several of its aspects: 'It would, of course, be grossly erroneous to exaggerate this truth and to extend it beyond certain fundamental features of our revolution. It would also be erroneous to lose sight of the fact that, soon after the victory of the proletarian revolution in at least one of the advanced countries, a sharp change will probably come about: Russia will cease to be the model and will once again become a backward country (in the "Soviet" and the socialist sense).' In a further passage he returns to the same question and says: 'It was easy for Russia, in the specific and historically unique situation of 1917, to *start* the socialist revolution, but it will be more difficult for Russia than for the European countries to *continue* the revolution and bring it to its consummation.'[29]

It can not be either the task or the purpose of the present discussion to present, even in an indicative and sketchy way, let alone to criticize, particular actions of the Soviet government. Yet it must be noted that Lenin saw the 'War Communism' period as an emergency measure enforced by circumstances, and considered the New Economic Policy as a transitional form brought about by the specific situation, whereas Stalin attributed all his attempts to reshuffle the distribution of the population in a capitalistically backward country by force, to a general prototype for any socialist development. In contrast to Lenin, he declared the Soviet development to be a classical one. It therefore became impossible, so long as this conception prevailed, to evaluate the important experiences of Soviet development correctly, from a theoretical point of view, and thus also fruitfully; for the correctness or falsity of any particular step can only be adequately assessed in the context of this non-classical development. The declaration of 'classicism' impeded an investigation of this path to socialism, which was so significant internationally, and put all discussion about internal reforms, etc. on the wrong track.

What is perhaps even more important for the Marxist theory of history is the question of uneven development which has already been mentioned. In his fragmentary notes at the end of the Introduction to the *Grundrisse,* Marx deals with this 'unequal relation' principally in the connection between economic development and such important social objectifications as law and especially art. Here he immediately stresses a decisive ontological and methodological aspect that must be placed in the centre of any consideration of problems of this kind: the concept of progress: 'In general, the concept of progress is not to be conceived in the usual abstractness.'[30] The first point, in this connection, is therefore to break with the abstraction of a too general concept of progress; in the last analysis, this concept is an application of the projection extrapolated from logic and epistemology to the historical process of an absolutely generalized reason. We already noted in considering essence and appearance how, in Marx's conception, objective economic progress may inevitably have a reducing and distorting effect on the general development of human capacities—although of course only temporarily. Here, too, we are dealing with an important case of uneven development, although this is treated methodologically by Marx only implcitly, and not expressly as appertaining to this. The question involves an unevenness in the development of human abilities as a result of the economically conditioned process by which the categories of social being become ever more social. Indirectly, there is always a reference to qualitative changes in this connection: the observations of a primitive hunter can in no way be directly compared with those of an experimental natural scientist of today. Consideration of abstractly isolated particular fields leads us to a complicated counterposing of increases and decreases in powers of observation, so that any individual progress in one respect must necessarily arise simultaneously with regressions in another respect. Culture criticism based on philosophical romanticism generally starts with these regressions, which are undoubtedly present, and uses this measure to contest the presence of any progress. On the other hand we have the rise, to an ever greater degree, of a vulgarized and simplifying conception of progress, which is based purely on any available already quantified end-product of the development

119

(growth of the productive forces, quantitative expansion of knowledge, etc.) and decrees a general progress on this foundation. In both cases, aspects which are important, but which are only particular aspects of the overall process, are blown up into the sole criterion; this leads to a failure to recognize the essence of the question, and the not unjustified criticism of one of these methods can even make it appear plausible that there is no ultimate answer to this problem.

It could perhaps be objected here that what is involved is simply a contradiction in the relation between appearance and essence, which could not exert a decisive influence on the objectively necessary advance of the essence. This would however be superficial, although it is correct that, in the last analysis, the ontological line of development of social being is maintained throughout all these contradictions. But since this progress is inseparably bound up with human capacities, it can not be a matter of indifference, even from the standpoint of purely objective and categorical progress, whether it produces an adequate or a distorted world of appearance. However, the question is still not by a long way settled. We know that the objective ontological movement towards the highest level of sociality of this being is the result of human actions, and if the individual decisions that men make between alternatives in the progress of the totality do not produce the individually envisaged results, this does not mean that the end product of this joint action is in any way completely independent of these individual acts. This relationship, in its general form, must be formulated very carefully, for the dynamic connection just mentioned between the individual acts based on the choice of alternatives and the overall movement shows a great variation in history; it differs between the various social formations, and particularly with their different stages of development and transition. It is evidently impossible here even to attempt to indicate the innumerable variations in this connection. It may suffice to point out that on the one hand the importance of the positions taken up by human groups (which are of course syntheses of individual decisions) has a much greater objective weight in situations of revolutionary transition, than in periods of the peaceful consolidation of a formation. It follows naturally from this, too, that the social weight of individual decisions also increases. Lenin correctly described the social nature of such pivotal points in history: 'It is only when the *"lower classes" do not want* to live in the old way and the "upper classes" *cannot carry on in the old way* that the revolution can triumph.'[31] On the other hand it must be added here, precisely from the standpoint of uneven development, that not only are the objective and subjective factors clearly distinguishable in any revolutionary transformation—but—and this is the objective basis for this distinction—they in no way necessarily run parallel, but may rather have different directions, tempos, intensities, and levels of consciousness, etc., according to their complicated social determinations. It is also a well-founded ontological fact that there can be objectively revolutionary situations that remain unresolved because the subjective factor has not sufficiently matured, just as popular explosions are possible that are not backed by sufficient objective elements of crisis. We need not expand in detail on the fact that this situation forms an important aspect of the unevenness in social and historical development. We only need think of the two occasions in modern Germany in which the subjective factor was lacking (1848 and 1918).

The fact that Marx does not mention the problem we have just indicated in the methodological remarks in his Introduction does not mean that it does not form, in his method, part of the complex of questions of uneven development. What Marx focussed his attention on there were special constellations that seemed paradoxical to an undialectical viewpoint and were not otherwise discussed, and he left unmentioned what appeared to him as obvious.[32] It is the same with the brief reference that we are here in the process of making with respect to unevenness in general economic development. It is flatly self-evident that the conditions of economic development vary between different countries. But the role that this unevenness plays in reality is often surprising, and is even an overwhelming transformative one. Just to take one extremely well-known example, we need only think of the revolutionary reshuffling of the whole economic balance in Europe as a result of the discovery of America and the resulting transformation of all trade routes. The decisive fact here is that the economic development again and again, one could even say continuously, creates new situations, in which the human groups involved (from tribes through to nations) have both objectively and subjectively very different aptitudes for realizing, elaborating and furthering them. This means that the relative and very often extremely precarious balance between them must be time and again upset; the rise of one and the decline of the other often gives the overall development a completely changed appearance.[33]

These elementary facts of economic life, which range from geographical situation[34] through to the internal distribution of population, and whose mobility or rigidity can lend different elements of a given situation the decisive significance, have an existential presence with the very rise of society and economic production. Because they are an essential part of social being, they realize their actuality only in parallel with the retreat of the natural boundary, as the social structure and its dynamic forces become ever more purely social. This tendency increases with the real economic intricacy of the economic realm. Rome and China had quite different economic developments, but since they scarcely exerted any influence whatsoever on one another, it is hardly possible to ascribe this difference to uneven development; or at most one could say, in Hegelian fashion, that uneven development was already present in itself, without having yet been realized for itself. Capitalist production, as the first genuinely social production, is thus also the first suitable terrain for the genuine evolution of uneven development. This is simply because the economic linkage of ever larger and economically more diversely structured territories creates a system of ever richer and more intricate economic relations, within which local variations—in the positive as well as the negative sense—can influence ever more easily and more intensely the direction of the overall development. The fact that these variations in the tempo of economic development time and again culminate in political and military actions, still further increases the force of this tendency to unevenness. Lenin was therefore quite right in treating this question as a focal point in his analysis of the imperialist period.[35] In uneven development, the ontological heterogeneity of the components of any complex or relation of complexes finds its expression; the more developed and social is the economy, the more strongly do the heterogeneities of the natural elements fall into the background, and are transformed more and more purely in the direction of sociality. This process, however, only suspends the natural character, and not the heterogeneities themselves. The latter must certainly be synthesized in the unity of the overall stream—and the more so, the more strongly social categories develop—but their originally heterogenous character remains within this synthesis, and produces tendencies of uneven development within the general laws of the overall process. Thus these do not involve an opposition to general historicity in the area of the economy itself, let alone a historicist 'uniqueness' or irrationality of the overall process, but they rather form a necessary mode of appearance that results out of the characteristic of social being.

We can now go into the questions of uneven development

discussed methodologically by Marx himself in somewhat more detail. The main question here is that of art, but Marx also mentions, and even with special emphasis as 'the really difficult point', 'how relations of production develop unevenly as legal relations.'[36] Unfortunately these fragmentary sketches do not even intimate how Marx conceives the methodological solution to this problem. Fortunately for us, Marx came back to this question in his criticism, in a letter, of Lassalle's *System der erworbenen Rechte* ['system of acquired rights'], and Engels also left some relevant notes in his letter to Conrad Schmidt. Here, the possibility of an uneven development is seen as arising on the basis of the social division of labour. So long as the problems of social collaboration and coexistence were essentially ordained by custom, so long as men themselves were in a position to decide their spontaneously arising and easily perceivable needs without a special apparatus (family and domestic slaves; law in direct democracies), the problem of an independence of the legal sphere from the economic did not even emerge. It was only a higher level of social development, with the rise of class differentiation and class antagonism, that the necessity arose of creating special organs, institutions, etc. for the regulation of the economic, social, etc. intercourse between men. As soon as these different spheres came into being, their mode of functioning, although the product of specific teleological projects that were determined by the basic conditions of life of the society in question (by the strata that were at the time decisive), nevertheless stood for this very reason in a relationship of heterogeneity towards the latter. This is nothing new from a social point of view; in analysing labour we shall have to deal in detail with the ontologically necessary heterogeneities that are necessarily present in any teleological project, simply between end and means. At the level of society as a concrete totality there is a similar relationship between economy and law, though one that is still more complicated in its structure. In particular, the heterogeneity is still more acute. For what is involved here is not simply heterogeneity within one and the same teleological project, but rather heterogeneity between two different systems of teleological projects. Law is in fact still more decisively a project than is the sphere and acts of economics, since it is only in a relatively developed society that there arises a conscious reinforcement of relations of domination, a regulation of economic intercourse, etc. It follows from this alone that the starting-point of this teleological project must have a character radically different to that of the economic. In contrast to the economy, it is not designed to bring about anything materially new; it rather presupposes this whole world as existing, and attempts to build into it binding principles of order that could not develop out of its immanent spontaneity.

Here, too, it cannot be our task to depict the heterogeneity of these two types of social project in its concrete form. The great differences between economic formations and the systems of law to which these give rise would lead us far from our proper problem. What we had to do was simply to point out the general characteristics of this heterogeneity, in order to arrive at a better understanding of the Marxian conception of uneven development in this area. What Marx particularly indicates in the letter to Lassalle which we have already mentioned, is 'that the *legal* conception of particular property relationships, for all that this grows out of these, is nevertheless not congruent with them, and cannot be congruent with them.'[37] Our earlier remarks have already indicated how this impossibility of congruency that Marx stresses should not be understood in an epistemological sense. Such an approach to the problem would make this incongruency into a mere lack, and the establishment of the congruency would be a demand to find or establish the congruency of ideas, whereas Marx has in mind an ontological social situation in which this

125

congruency is impossible on principle, because of a mode of appearance of social practice in general which, for better or worse, as the case may be, can only function precisely on the basis of incongruency. Marx goes on directly to deal with uneven development. He shows in particular that in the continuity of historical development the attempts to grasp a legal phenomenon in thought and to transform it into practice are time and again conducted in the form of regression to institutions from earlier eras and their interpretation, and in fact must be so conducted. But these are nevertheless received and applied in a manner that in no way corresponds to the original meaning of the tradition, and which assumes its misunderstanding. Hence Marx says in an apparently paradoxical way against Lassalle: 'You have shown how the adoption of the Roman code. . . originally rested on a misunderstanding. But it in no way follows from this that the code in its *modern* form. . . is the *misunderstood* Roman code. It could in that case be said that every achievement of an earlier era that is taken over by a later one is the *misunderstood old one.* . . The misunderstood form is precisely the general form, and the form which at a certain stage of social development can be turned to general use.'[38] Here it is still more evident that this misunderstanding can as little be interpreted epistemologically as can the earlier incongruency. What is involved is a specific social need, and the intention to fulfil this in what is at the time an optimal way, by means of a teleological project of a kind whose prerequisites we have just described. This is based to a higher degree on the choice of alternatives than are economic acts, since here aim and means are not even relatively given in the material immediacy, and the creation of a homogenous medium *sui generis* is required for aim and means to become practical, as the necessary basis for the social task to be fulfilled.

Another point that follows from this, and which makes this situation still more acute, is that the social task generally requires for its fulfilment a system whose criteria, at least in a formal sense, can neither be derived from the task itself nor from its material foundation, but must be specific, internal and immanent. What this means in our case is that a legal regulation of human social intercourse requires a specific and juridically homogenized ideal system of rules, etc., whose construction ultimately depends on the 'incongruency' that Marx established between this realm of ideas and the economic reality.

This also expresses a basic structural fact of social development that we shall come to analyse in our discussion of labour in its simplest and most elementary characteristics: the means of realization of a teleological project possess—within specific limits which will immediately be indicated—a specific and immanent dialectical connection, and the internal perfection of this is one of the most important moments for successful realization of the project. The most various means and mediations of social life must therefore be co-ordinated in such a way as to achieve this immanent perfection, which in the area of law is of a formal and homogenizing kind. Yet however important the role of this in the overall process, and hence also of an adequate understanding of it, it is still only one aspect of the real state of affairs. For it is equally certain that not every immanent perfection can attain the same degree of social effectiveness. The formal closure of a system of arrangements of this kind may stand in an incongruent relationship to the material that has to be arranged, as the reflection of this, but certain of its actual essential elements still have to be correctly grasped both in thought and in practice if it is to be able to perform its regulating function. This criterion combines two heterogenous moments, i.e. a material and a teleological. In the case of labour this appears as the necessary unification of the technological and the economic moment, in the case of law as the immanent juridical coherence and consistency in its relationship with the political and social goals of the legal system. This gives rise to a conceptual division in this teleological project, which is often formulated in terms of a duality between the origin of law and the legal system, with the point that the origin of law is not legal in character. This division appears so sharp that the major representative exponent of legal formalism, Kelsen, occasionally even described legislation as a 'mystery'.[39] It is relevant here that the teleological project of the origin of law is necessarily the result of a struggle between heterogenous social forces (classes), regardless of whether this struggle is carried through to its ultimate consequences, or whether it results in a compromise between the classes.

If we go back now to the extremely important historic case adduced by Marx, where something handed down from an earlier period is actualized, it is clear that any project of this kind must have a very complicated internal 'prehistory', and that many alternatives at various levels must have been adopted, before a legal system endowed with a unitary and homogenous mode of functioning can be achieved. It is only this situation that gives the case dealt with by Marx, of regression to the past, and his conception of the 'mis-understanding', a comprehensible social significance. The re-interpretation of the past arises primarily from the needs of the present; an epistemological objective identity or con-vergence can in no way provide the decisive motive for choice or rejection; this motive consists in an actual applicability in concrete present circumstances, from the standpoint of a resultant in the struggle between concrete social interests. The fact that the result of such a process must necessarily affect the development of the economy itself in an uneven way thus appears as a necessary result of the structural foundations of social development itself. But if this unevenness has to be presented as necessary, as against an impermissible logical rationalization and unification of the historical process, it is also necessary to take up a position against any conception that uses this as a basis for rejecting any regularity, in an empiricist of irrationalist fashion. Despite all the complicated syntheses of heterogenous components—in the ontological sense—uneven development is still law-like. The fact that individual decisions among alternatives may be simply false or harmful to development in no way alters this characteristic regularity at the level of the overall process.[40] Uneven development 'simply' means that the main line in the movement of social being, the increasing sociality of all categories, connections and relationships, cannot develop in a rectilinear fashion, according to some kind of rational 'logic', but that it develops partly by detours (even leaving behind blind alleys), and partly in such a way that the individual complexes whose combined movements are what composes the overall development must stand towards each other in a relationship of non-correspondence. But these deviations from the main line of the law-like overall development are based without exception on ontologically necessary circumstances. If these are accordingly investigated and discovered, then the lawfulness and necessity of deviations of this kind becomes visibly apparent; it is just that they must be analysed in terms of the ontologically operative facts and relations. We already quoted Marx's decisive methodological remark for analyses of this kind: 'The difficulty consists only in the general formulation of these contradictions. As soon as they have been specified, they are already clarified.'[41]

The second problem of uneven development that Marx deals with here is that of art. If we want to do justice to Marx's conception, we must immediately stress that the conditions of unevenness are qualitatively and radically distinct here from those of law which have so far been discussed. This point precisely corresponds to the methodological remark that has just been quoted for the second time. Here, again, it is necessary to concretely elaborate the social components which determine the particular phenomenon of artistic development. In the fragmentary sketches that we are discussing here, Marx proceeds from the concrete social characteristic of the society on whose basis the work of art being investigated arises. In this connection he breaks immediately—we could even say in advance—with two prejudices that have constantly led to Marx's method being compromised by his so-called followers. Firstly, with the conception that the genesis of the work of art, which certainly belongs to the superstructure, can therefore be simply and directly derived from the economic base. Marx, on the contrary, proceeds from 'the starting-point of the whole society, including its ideological tendencies (naturally, here in a deliberately most abbreviated fashion); the latter are even given a specially strong emphasis in the example of Homer that Marx adduces, in so far as Homer's art is brought into an inseparable relationship with Greek mythology, and it is expressly emphasized that Homer's art would have been impossible in the historical context of a different mythology, let alone in an era without mythology. If anyone else but Marx was involved, the vulgarizers would certainly have reproached him with neglecting the economic base. In Marx's case, we can see that he conceived social being as determined by 'mythologizing relations' as well as by the economic structure of the time. What Marx means here, however, is far more than simply a rejection of vulgarization. On the one hand he relates art to the totality of social relations, while on the other hand he sees that the intention of a work of art, an artist or a type of art cannot be oriented to the extensive totality of all social relations, but that a choice has had to be made, from objective necessity, in so far as specific moments of the totality are of predominant importance for a specific artistic project, as in Homer the specific form of Greek mythology.

In the second place, the demonstration of the genesis is not a matter of a simple causal nexus between base and superstructure (in this case art). The causal connection is of course always there; but what is of decisive significance for the Marxist concept of genesis is whether this kind of determinacy is favourable or unfavourable for the rise of an art-form.[42] In the sketches that we are investigating here, Marx sets his sights directly at uneven development itself. He proceeds from the fact as from something generally known and acknowledged: 'In the case of the arts, it is well known that certain periods of their flowering are out of all proportion to the general development of society, hence also to the material foundation, the skeletal structure as it were, of its organization.' With respect to Homer, and also to Shakespeare, Marx asserts that 'certain significant forms within the realm of the arts are possible only at an undeveloped stage of artistic development.' And he adds: 'If this is the case with the relation between different kinds of art within the realm of the arts, it is already less puzzling that it is the case in the relation of the entire realm to the general development of society.'[43] This leads to the sentence that we have already quoted twice on the question of the general conception of this question and the special fruitfulness of specification.

Uneven development is thus in Marx's eyes a well-established fact, and the task of science is that of explaining its conditions, causes, etc. The decisive approach to this is already accomplished in these fragmentary sketches, in so far as Marx indicates, in the context of the integral totality of a society, how each individual work of art, as a result of its particular properties, stands in a particular relationship to certain moments of this totality, and how the form and content of this relationship are concretely decisive in influencing its particular development. We repeat that this can only take place in the general context of the overall development, the stage it has reached at the time, and the corresponding prevailing tendencies. But since the question of the favourable or unfavourable conditions of the work of art arises with inherent necessity in connection with every one of these moments, and particularly in connection with that with which the work of art in question is particularly and intimately associated, the unevenness of its development is given simultaneously with the mere existence of art. From this point of view, Marx's stress on Greek mythology as the decisive factor for the rise of the Homeric epic has a methodological significance which goes beyond the concrete explanation of this particular phenomenon. For Marx thereby indicates the specific social phenomenon whose presence or absence, its what and how, has a decisive importance both for the rise of the epic itself and for its development, as the favourable or unfavourable condition of the social environment. (We can compare the role of mythology in Virgil and later epic poetry as well as the similar form of poetry of the Orient.) Unfortunately this methodological suggestion of Marx's found little response among his successors; even Plekhanov and Mehring dealt with artistic phenomena predominantly in an abstractly sociological way, and in the Stalin era there arose a quite mechanical reduction, a complete indifference towards the independent and uneven development of artistic forms. If I may refer to my own work here, for methodological reasons, I sought to show for example how, for the reasons adduced here by Marx, the same capitalist development led to an upswing of music that had no previous precedent, while for architecture it was the source of a constantly developing problem that became ever more difficult to resolve.[44]

It is part of the ontological nature of social being that all the directions, tendencies, etc. that appear in it are made up of individual acts of an alternative nature. In the arts, where the overwhelming majority of objectifications that have to be considered are directly the product of individual acts, this general structure must attain a particular importance, i.e. the law of uneven development here affects the individual acts themselves in a still more profound and decisive fashion. The general ontological basis for this phenomenon is known and recognized: the fact already noted by Hegel, that human actions have results different from those envisaged in their subjective goals, and that therefore—speaking very roughly and generally—men usually make history with a false consciousness. In the course of development of Marxism, this point became reduced to an essentially polemical instrument of politics: the exposure of the opponent by way of a criticism—predominantly based on epistemological grounds—of the non-agreement between his ideology and his actions. Without wanting to go into this question in detail, as to when, where and to what extent this practice agreed with Marx's own conception, we must once again indicate that Marx himself never treated this question simply from the standpoint of epistemology, but rather always ontologically. It follows from this that he not only critically exposed the negative results of inadequacies of this kind, which he did very often, but also pointed out important cases of world-historically necessary and hence fruitful ideological 'self-deceptions', which helped men to carry out great deeds which they would otherwise have found impossible.[45]

The phenomenon that we are investigating here certainly has this general 'false consciousness' as its ontological foundation, but it essentially goes far beyond this. What happens here is that an artist who shares the 'false consciousness' of his age, his nation and his class, is able in certain circumstances, when his artistic practice is confronted with reality, to break out of the world of his prejudices and to conceive the real world in its genuine and profound characteristics; the fact that he *can* do this in certain circumstances does not of course mean that he necessarily *has* to do so. Marx himself already noted this phenomenon in his youth. In his criticism of Eugène Sue he speaks of a successful character in his novel and says that here Sue 'has risen above the horizon of his narrow world out-

look. He has slapped bourgeois prejudice in the face.'[46] Many
decades later Engels formulated this ideological relationship in
more detail and more precisely in a letter to Mary Harkness:
'The realism I allude to, may crop out even in spite of the
author's opinions.' And after analysing this phenomenon in
the case of Balzac, he summarizes his ideas as follows. 'That
Balzac thus was compelled to go against his own class
sympathies and political prejudices, that he *saw* the necessity
of the downfall of his favourite nobles, and described them as
people deserving no better fate; and that he *saw* the real men
of the future where, for the time being, they alone were to be
found—that I consider one of the greatest triumphs of
Realism, and one of the grandest features of old Balzac.'[47]

It is not the place here to go into the significance of this
point for the understanding of art and its history in more detail.
I have myself sought to apply it and make it more concrete
in various studies. Here, too, few words are needed to explain
that the whole Marxian theory of the uneven development of
the arts was and remained abhorrent to the 'monolithic
ideology of Stalinism.' For our own basic problem, it simply
has to be noted that this significantly concretizes and deepens
in a dialectical sense Marx's correct concept of the favourable
or unfavourable character of a period for art (for specific
forms of art). It is clear in particular that within this favourable or unfavourableness, which, even if it is more precisely
differentiated in respect to particular forms of art, still
remains a general social category, there can be and actually
are still further individual alternatives for particular artists. In
this way the uneven development reappears at a higher
dialectical level, in so far as in an unfavourable period it is still
possible for important works of art to be produced. This
certainly does not abolish the unfavourableness—any attempt
to do so would certainly lead to vulgarizing simplifications—
but it brings to light the fact that a further uneven development of a higher power is possible within the original. (The

converse is of course also true, that favourable circumstances can in no way provide a guarantee for a flowering of art.)

Even though this presentation is fragmentary (and it has to be so, if we are not inadequately to forestall questions that we shall come to deal with only in the second part of this work, or even only in the Ethics), it cannot be concluded without at least raising an ontological problem of the general development of social being, which involves a new aspect both of the historicity of this, and of objective progress within it: the problem of the human race. Already in his early work Marx rejected the static and naturalistic exegesis of this question by Feuerbach, which excluded consideration of the totality. He wrote in his sixth thesis on Feuerbach that, as a result of his basically false conception, Feuerbach was forced: '1. To abstract from the historical process and to define the religious sentiment by itself, and to presuppose an abstract—*isolated*—individual. 2. Essence, therefore, can be regarded only as "species", as an inner, mute, general character which unites the many individuals *in a natural way*.'[40] The false extremes that Feuerbach's conception gives rise to are thus on the one hand the isolated, abstract individual, and on the other hand the natural muteness of the genus.

With this we find ourselves once again at the centre of the specificity of social being. It is a commonplace that organic life brings forth species. But in the last analysis it only produces species, for the individual organisms that really and directly embody the species come and go, and only the species remains constant in this change—at least as long as it remains itself. The connection that thus arises between organism and species is a purely natural one, quite independent of any consciousness or any conscious objectification: the species is realized in the individual organisms, and the latter in their life process realize the species. It is self-evident that the species can have no consciousness of its own; and it is just as self-evident that no species-consciousness managed to arise in the natural organism. This is certainly not because the higher animals have no consciousness, an idea that has long since been refuted by experience and by science. It is rather because the real production and reproduction of their life does not create for them any kind of relation through which the two-fold unity of organism and species could acquire an objective expression. It is plain that only labour can provide this decisive moment, of course with all the consequences that it involves for the behaviour of men towards their environment, to nature and to their fellow creatures. The young Marx repeatedly describes this distinction between man and animal, always on the basis of labour and the phenomena arising from it. Thus in the *German Ideology* he refers to the development of speech from the needs of human intercourse, and says about animals: 'Where there exists a relationship, it exists for me: the animal does not 'relate' itself to anything, it does not 'relate' at all. For the animal, its relation to others does not exist as a relation.'[49] Similarly in the *Economic and Philosophical Manuscripts,* where the effects of exchange between men are investigated, and it is pointed out that it is only in this way that the differentiation of men becomes an important and valuable moment of social intercourse. In the animals, on the other hand: 'The particular qualities of the different races within a species of animal are by nature more marked than the differences between human aptitudes and activities. But since animals are not able to *exchange,* the diversity of qualities in animals of the same species but of different races does not benefit any individual animal. Animals are unable to combine the different qualities of their species; they are incapable of contributing anything to the *common* good and the *common* comfort of their species.'[50] These and similar differences give a very concrete and differentiated content to the assertion that the species, as a relation of mere biological viability, can only have a dumb generality.

The other reproach against Feuerbach, that he only considered the isolated individual and not the concrete (social) man, seems at first glance not to follow the same situation. But this is only an appearance, although this objection of Marx's is not directed backwards, as a comparison with the purely biological species-being of animals, but rather forwards, to a society with a highly developed division of labour, in which the linkage between the individual and his species-being can get lost from consciousness. In the normal case, it is labour that originally creates this connection. Marx also says in the *Economic and Philosophical Manuscripts:* 'It is therefore in his fashioning of the objective that man really proves himself to be a *species-being.* Such production is his active species-life. Through it nature appears as *his* work and his reality. The object of labour is therefore the *objectification of the species-life of man:* for man reproduces himself not only intellectually, in his consciousness, but actively and actually, and he can therefore contemplate himself in a world he has created.'[51] In a further passage from the same work, Marx draws the consequences of the above: 'The individual *is* the social being. His vital expression—even when it does not appear in the direct form of a *communal* expression, conceived in association with other men—is therefore an expression and confirmation of *social life*.'[52] What one is accustomed to call the isolated individual involves a particular state of consciousness within a human sociality that is fundamentally objective as well as subjective. The ontological position that man, in so far as he is man, is a social being, and that in every act of his life, no matter how this may be reflected in his consciousness, he always and without exception realizes himself, in a contradictory way, together with the stage of development reached at the time by the human species, even if he does this in the most various ways, is not a thesis first put forward by Marx. This fundamental truth was concretely repeated and decisively stressed from Aristotle through to Goethe and Hegel; it is sufficient perhaps to look at one of Goethe's last conversations, in which he stresses against Soret the absolutely unavoidable character of the interconnection between the individual and society in any expression whatsoever of his life, with great stress on his own life experience.[53]

It is a fact of cultural history that in at least relatively highly developed societies, and especially frequently in times of crisis, the idea develops in particular individuals that all relations of the individual to society are merely external, secondary, and merely supplementary, are ultimately established artificially, and can be terminated or abolished at will. From the hermits of the first centuries of Christianity, through to Heidegger's doctrine of 'thrownness', it plays an indelible role, as one might say, in the history of thought. From the classical Robinsonades, through to what I have called in my criticism of existentialism the Robinsonades of decadence, this conception still dominates a considerable part of bourgeois ideology; it has even obtained a pseudo-ontological foundation, with the aid of the transformed modern Christian tradition of Kierkegaard, and the ostensible precision of Husserlian phenomenology: i.e. that it is the isolated individual that is ontologically primary and the basis of everything in the human world. It is of course possible, with the aid of a 'phenomenology', to conceive all human relations as derived in this way, as created by the isolated individual and hence to be understood by reducing them back to him. And it is in accordance with this method—which really does put the world 'in brackets'—to abolish the difference between the given, which is ontologically primary, and the subjective reflexes to this given, to present the effect as the foundation and vice versa. This does not however affect the fundamental facts. Shaw, for example, showed very wittily in one of his comedies how the rentiers feel themselves to be very 'free' and 'undetermined' by society, and how reality reminds them with a great shock of how massively social the foundations of their 'independence' have been. In the *Grundrisse,* in criticizing the original Robinsonades, Marx takes issue with this prejudice:

'The more deeply we go back into history, the more does the individual, and hence also the producing individual, appear as dependent, as belonging to a greater whole: in a still quite natural way in the family and in the family expanded into the clan *[Stamm];* then later in the various forms of communal society arising out of the antithesis and fusions of the clans. Only in the eighteenth century, in "civil society", do the various forms of social connectedness confront the individual as a mere means towards his private purposes, as external necessity. But the epoch which produces this standpoint, that of the isolated individual, is also precisely that of the hitherto most developed social (form this standpoint, general) relations. The human being is in the most literal sense a *zoon politikon,* not merely a gregarious animal, but an animal which can individuate itself only in the midst of society.'[54] In attacking the imaginary characteristics of the isolated individual, a mere product of consciousness, Marx always harks back to the major questions of social theory. In the last analysis, the point is that it is not individuals who 'construct' society, but rather that individuals, on the contrary, arise in society and from the development of society, and that—to repeat once again something that has frequently been stressed—the real complex therefore has ontological priority over its components. In *The Holy Family* Marx argues in a similar vein against the Left Hegelian (and general liberal) conception according to which the isolated individual is the 'atom', and the mass of atoms is 'held together' by the state. On the contrary, the state is only erected on the foundations of the society, and the 'atoms' exist and operate within this, always as governed by its real properties.[55]

Leaving this false problem behind, and turning back to the genuine relationship between individual and species, we see that the realization of the species-character in the individual is inseparable from the real relations in which the individual produces and reproduces his own existence, and thus inseparable from the development of individuality itself. This has decisive structural and historical consequences for the whole problem. In the 'mute' connection between the animal and his species, the connection remains purely 'in itself', and accordingly is perpetually related to itself and realizes itself in a pure and abstract form in the individual examples; the behaviour of the individual remains unchanged in this form of species-character, as long as the species itself remains phylogenetically unchanged.

Now since the connection of man to his species has from the beginning been formed and mediated by way of social categories such as labour, speech, exchange, commerce, etc., and since it is on principle never 'mute', but can only be realized in consciously operative relations and connections, concrete partial realities thus arise within a human species that at first existed in a similar 'in itself' fashion, and which take over the place of this 'in itself' in the development of species-consciousness precisely as a result of their concrete partiality and particularity. It is thus also relevant that the natural biological general species-character of man, which exists in itself and must insuperably persist in this form, can only realize itself as the human species, that the existing social complexes are always operative in their very concrete partiality and particularity, and that the 'dumbness' of the species-being is overcome by the members of a society of this kind, in so far as they become conscious of their species-character, in the context of this complex, and as members of it. The fundamental objective contradiction in this relationship is expressed in the fact that the species' attainment of consciousness in this partiality and particularity more or less completely conceals the general species-being, or at least pushes it a long way into the background. Just as specifically human consciousness can only arise in connection with, and as the result of, the social activity of men, so the consciousness of membership of the species grows up out of their concrete coexistence and cooperation. The result of this is that what at first appears as the species is in no way humanity itself, but rather the temporary concrete human society in which men live, work, and have concrete intercourse with one another. For these reasons alone, the rise of human species-consciousness displays the most varied stages and orders of magnitude, from the still almost naturally connected clans up to the great nations.

This contradiction is still not fully depicted with the establishment of this basic phenomenon. What must be kept in mind above all is that ever since the dissolution of primitive communism, the social complexes that were the subject of consideration could no longer have an internally unified character: classes had arisen. It is not our task to portray this development, even in a rough sketch. It must just be noted that the pluralist and dynamic internal property that a complex of this kind thereby acquired, displays the greatest variations in the course of history, and often of a mutually contrary character. Thus the caste system has a tendency towards static stabilization of the complexes it embraces, whereas the most developed and most purely social form of this structure, the class division, operates as a rule in a dynamic and forward-driving direction. Although this structure is inherent to any concrete social complex, it would be a crude oversight from the standpoint of our problem if we did not take cognizance of the fact that these two systems of formation of the human social community stand to one another in a relationship of competition, even if the symptoms of this only reveal themselves clearly in acute form in times of crisis. History is full of alliances in which particular classes join with foreign states against their class enemies. This is of course based on the fact that men very often only experience their state or society as their own in the context of a specific class domination. This demonstrates the concrete character of species-consciousness in society. While the dumb, biological species is something purely objective, unchangeable from the standpoint of the individual organism, the relationship of man to the social complex in which he realizes his species-consciousness is one of activity, collaboration, construction or destruction. This is why the feeling of belonging to a concrete community, or at least habituation to it, forms the indispensable pre-condition for the rise of the species in the social sense. This does not of course mean that the question is purely one of consciousness. Consciousness is first and foremost the form of reaction to various socially objective concrete relationships (certainly a reaction of an alternative character), and the space in which the alternatives of the moment present themselves is also objectively limited by economic and social factors. Consciousness is the reaction of the individual, often unclear and simply on the basis of feelings, to the social environment which exists for him as a given existence.

Without dealing in detail here with concrete variants, stages, etc., a simple glance at the general course of development indicates the tendency towards constant growth of these complexes, even if this is certainly uneven, and full of regressions. Here, too, we do not need to give examples. It is an uncontestable fact that the earth was once populated by a countless number of small tribes, which were frequently almost unaware of their own neighbours, while it is now on the way to forming an economic unity, a comprehensive and all-sided interdependence of the most far-removed peoples. What is important for us in this respect is simply that this integration is accomplished by economic development generally without the knowledge of the participants, and more than frequently against their will. The spontaneous and unstayable unification of men into a human race which is no longer dumb, no longer simply a natural species, is thus a further necessary accompaniment of the development of the productive forces. We have shown that this development inevitably leads to an increase in the capacities of individual men; this progress is supplemented by the process indicated here, which brings about the rise of the human species. It must also be stressed in this connection that this, too, is meant in a purely ontological sense, as the way towards the human species in the social sense, as the transformation of the natural 'in itself' into a being 'for us', and even—in prospect—into its fullest development into a being 'for itself'. This purely ontological consideration therefore does not involve any kind of value judgement, any kind of reference to socially objective values. Of course, this development involves various necessary forms of socially objective values being posited, just as did the former aspect, the higher development of human abilities. But these are questions which we shall only be able to go into in detail at a far more concrete stage of knowledge of sociality. What is decisive here is simply the indubitable ontological fact that the development of the productive forces must necessarily accomplish this progress: just as labour brought about the transformation of animal into man, right at the beginning of its realization, so its permanent further development brings about the rise of the human species in its properly social sense.

In order not to let any misunderstandings arise in connection with this simple establishment of an ontological fact, even if a fundamental one, a few additional remarks are necessary. Firstly, this process is in no way a teleological one. All transformations in the natural connections between men themselves and between them and nature which lead in the direction of sociality are brought about as a result of spontaneous changes in the economic reality; all that happens according to law is that, despite many stagnations and regressions, the general tendency of the economic accomplishes a rise in the sociality of the forms of human intercourse, as well as a simultaneous integration of smaller communities into ever more extensive and comprehensive ones, and that the joining together of various social complexes, both extensively and intensively, is constantly on the increase. Capitalism finally creates a *de facto* world economy, for the first time in history, in which every human society is linked economically with all others. The rise of the human species in the social sense is the unintended but necessary product of the development of the productive forces. Secondly, and this reinforces still more the non-teleological character of this advance, we also have to refer to uneven development in this connection. Not all formations have the same tendency towards their own re-production on an extended scale. Marx shows for example in the case of the so-called Asiatic relations of production that the tendency of their economic base was towards simple reproduction.[56] Hence we have the formation of what from the point of view of our progression are blind alleys, which only come to an end eventually, after long periods of stagnation, with the penetration of capitalism, a destruction of the old economic forms that comes from without. The ancient slave economy also came into a blind alley, though one of a completely different kind, and could only develop towards feudalism by way of a historical 'accident', i.e. the permeation of the Germanic migrations. Thirdly, the non-teleological character of this regular development is also shown from the fact that, just as with the increase in human abilities, the concrete vehicle of realization is in permanent contradiction to the thing itself: bloody wars, enslavement, even extermination of whole peoples, devastation and human degradation, intensification of the relations between people to the point of centuries of hatred—these are the direct 'means' with the aid of which this integration of mankind into a species has taken place and is still taking place.

The fact remains, however, that the process still takes

place, just as it does in the case of the development of human abilities. The world history that first demonstrates itself as a social reality at this stage of development is itself a category of a historical character. Marx writes in the *Grundrisse:* 'World history has not always existed; history as world history a result.'[57] It does not contradict this ontological fact, but rather confirms it, that historical science is today already on the way to discovering and depicting the process that brought about this situation, and that there are thus already today the beginnings of a science of world history. For this world history can only find in science its own former ontological non-existence, in which of course, and this is most important to investigate, the process of integration of small unities into larger ones, if uneven, is nevertheless advancing, as well as the extensive and intensive constant growth in reciprocal intercourse, its influence on internal structures, etc. But world history as a social reality remains for all that a phenomenon of the most recent phase of development, for which it is characteristic, as a preparatory stage, that the subjective reactions of human beings and human groups in it are so often far removed from behaving in a manner appropriate to this objective situation, and even frequently display bitter opposition to it; the progress of events however shows that economic necessity must nevertheless be accomplished.

With the rise of a human species that is no longer dumb, we are faced with the same problem that we already confronted in establishing the fact of the development of human capacities and their contradictions (alienation etc.). The regular basic general line of the principal economic tendency is realized time and again in forms that not only display an unevenness in concrete development, not only reveal themselves in an internally contradictory manner, but stand in a direct relationship of contradiction to the decisive objective consequences of the regular principal development. This contradiction can only adequately be grasped from an ontological presentation of the totality of social development, its entire dynamic and regularity. Here, where we have to confine ourselves to one aspect of the Marxian ontology of social being (even if the central aspect), the ontological priority of the economic sphere, we can only anticipate the more concrete and detailed discussion that will follow later with some very general and highly abstract indications as to the real connections within the social totality. If we have conceived every society as a complex, we see that it consists, in an extremely intricate fashion, of heterogenous complexes which are thus heterogenous also in their effects; we need only refer here to the differentiation of antagonistic classes, or to the systems of mediation which erect themselves into relatively autonomous complexes (law, state, etc.). It should never be forgotten here that even these partial complexes themselves consist of complexes, human groups and individuals, whose reaction to their environment, which forms the foundation of all complexes of mediation and differentiation, insuperably involves decisions between alternatives.

At the first, direct glance, the interaction of all these dynamic forces seems to result in a chaos, or at least, a battle-field of values struggling against each other that is difficult to see as a whole, a battle-field, moreover, on which it seems hard for the individual, and at times even impossible, to find a conception of the world that will provide a foundation for his decisions between alternatives. Of all the thinkers of the recent past, it is Max Weber who has most clear-sightedly conceived this situation in its immediate form, and described it most transparently. In his essay *Science of a Vocation,* he writes: 'The impossibility of a "scientific" advocacy of practical attitudes. . . has a much deeper basis. It is fundamentally meaningless, because the various systems of values found in the world are locked in insoluble struggle with one another. . . If we know anything today, then we know that something can be holy not only despite its being unpleasant, but precisely *because* and *in so far as* it is unpleasant... and it is an everyday truth that something can be true, even though, and because, it is neither pleasant nor holy nor good... Here we are precisely confronted with the struggle of different gods with one another, and this is so for all time. It is like the old world, still not disenchanted of its gods and deamons, only in a different sense; just as the ancient Greek first gave a sacrifice to Aphrodite, then to Apollo, and particularly to all the gods of his own city, so it is still today, only without of the mythical garb of that behaviour, which however was in itself quite transparent. These gods and their struggles may well be governed by fate, but certainly not by any "science"... In his ultimate attitude, the individual takes one of these for the devil, and another for god, and it is the individual who has to decide which is god and which is devil *for him.* And this is how it goes right through all the orders of life... The many gods of old, now disenchanted and hence appearing in the form of impersonal powers, rise from their graves, strive for power over our lives, and begin once again their eternal battle.'[58]

The antinomies that are discussed here in the form of a tragic and pathetic scepticism continue to operate in later positions on this complex of problems, right through to today, the only difference being that they are cursed with the greater abstractness and superficiality of the related antipodes of neopositivism and existentialism. In the former this leads to a manipulative 'abolition' of all conflicts, in the latter, as a result of the displacement of all alternatives into the empty space of an abstract subjectivity, which does not even objectively exist in this abstract form, it leads to an internally hollow antinomy.

Traditional Marxism, however, can not make an end of these opponents. It has given rise to a false dualism of social being and social consciousness, which is based on epistemology, but for that very reason ignores the decisive ontological questions. It was Plekhanov, unquestionably the most philosophically educated theoretician of the pre-Leninist period, who, as far as I know, formulated this theory in the most influential way. He sought to define the relationship of base and superstructure in such a way that the former consisted of the 'state of the productive forces', and the 'economic relations these forces condition.' The 'socio-political system' arose on this base, already as a superstructure. It was only on this base that social consciousness arose, which Plekhanov defined as follows: 'a mentality which is determined in part directly by the economic conditions obtaining, and in part by the entire socio-political system that has arisen on that foundation.' Ideologies thus reflected 'the properties of that mentality.'[59] It is not hard to see that Plekhanov was here completely under the influence of nineteenth-century theories of knowledge. These essentially developed from the attempt to provide a philosophical foundation for the achievements of the modern natural sciences. Physics was understandably the decisive model here: on the one hand there was regularly determined being, in which there could be no question of the presence of consciousness, on the other hand the purely epistemic consciousness of the natural sciences, which did not seem to involve anything of an existential character in its functioning. Without dealing in detail with the problem of a pure theory of knowledge of this kind, the point has to be made here that this pure duality of being without consciousness and consciousness without being does have here a relative methodological justification, though only a relative one. Even the inclusion of organic life in the compass of this epistemology does not disturb the functioning of the model, since, as we have seen, the consciousness of the higher animals can still be considered as an epiphenomenon of their purely natural properties. It is only the application of this schema of the epistemological appearance to social being that gives rise to an unsolvable antinomy, which explodes this narrow framework. Bourgeois epistemology solves this question by a purely idealist interpretation of all social phenomena, in which the existential character of social being naturally as good as completely vanishes; this is even the case with N. Hartmann.

Marx's successors found themselves in a difficult situation in this respect. Since Marx correctly ascribed economic regularities a similarly general validity to that of natural laws, the idea suggested itself of applying these types of regularity, without further concretization or limitation, to social being in general. This led to a two-fold distortion of the ontological situation. Firstly, and very much against Marx's own conception, social being, and economic reality above all, appeared to be something purely natural (ultimately a being without consciousness); we saw how at a later stage consciousness in general appeared to Plekhanov as a problem. Marx's theory that the law-like economic results of individual teleological acts (thus acts involving consciousness) possess an objective regularity of their own has nothing in common with theories of this kind. A metaphysical contrast between social being and consciousness is diametrically opposed to Marx's ontology, in which all social being is inseparably linked with consciousness (with alternative projects). Secondly, and this concerns Plekhanov himself less than general vulgar Marxism, there arose a mechanistic and fatalist over-extension of economic necessity itself. This state of affairs is too well-known to need detailed criticism here; it should only be pointed out that the neo-Kantians' idea of 'supplementing' Marx is without exception related to these ideas and not to Marx's own positions. When Marx wrote in the Preface to *A Contribution to the Critique of Political Economy:* 'It is not the consciousness of men that determines their being, but, on the contrary, their social being that determines their consciousness',[60] this has nothing to do with theories of this kind. On the one hand, Marx does not counterpose social being to social consciousness, but to any consciousness. He does not recognize a specific social consciousness as a separate form. On the other hand, it follows from the first negative assertion that Marx was simply protesting here against idealism in this question, and was simply asserting the ontological priority of social being over consciousness.

Engels had a clear feeling that these vulgarizations were distorting Marxism. In letters that he wrote to important personalities in the workers' movement of the time, we find many indications to the effect that there are interactions between base and superstructure, that it would be pedantry to 'derive' individual historic facts simply from economic necessity, etc. He was quite right in all these questions, but he still did not always manage to refute these deviations from the Marxian method in a conclusive fashion. In his letters to Joseph Bloch and Franz Mehring, he certainly attempted to provide a theoretical foundation, even with a self-critical edge against his own and Marx's writings. Thus he wrote to Bloch: 'According to the materialist conception of history, the *ultimately* determining element in history is the pro- duction and reproduction of real life. More than this neither Marx nor I have ever asserted. Hence if somebody twists this into saying that the economic element is the *only* determining one, he transforms that proposition into a meaningless, abstract, senseless phrase. The economic situation is the basis, but the various elements of the superstructure. . . also exercise their influence upon the course of the historical struggles and in many cases preponderate in determining their *form*. There is an interaction of all these elements in which, amid all the endless host of accidents. . . the economic move- ment finally asserts itself as necessary.'[61]

There is no question but that Engels presents many essential features of this situation correctly, and very decisively corrects many errors of vulgarization. But where he seeks to give his criticism a philosophical foundation, I believe he clutches at a straw. For the additional opposition of content (economy) and form (superstructure) adequately expresses neither their connection nor their distinction. Even if we take from the letter to Mehring Engels' interpretation of the form as 'the ways and means by which these notions, etc., come about', we do not get much further. What Engels refers to here, and correctly, is the genesis of ideologies, and the relative specificity of this kind of genesis. This, too, however, cannot ultimately be understood as a relation of form and content. For this relationship, as we sought to show in the chapter on Hegel, is a reflection determination, which means that form and content ever and always, in the individual object, complex, process, etc., determine together and only together its specificity, its being as it is (including generality). But it is for this very reason impossible that in the determination of real and separate complexes to one another, the one should figure as content, and the other as form.

The difficulty of concluding this criticism of faulty interpretations of Marx with a positive rectification lies in the fact that at the highly abstract level of our discussions so far, the ontological prerequisites of the genuine and concrete dialectic of base and superstructure can not yet be developed, which is why an abstract anticipation can easily lead arouse misunderstandings. Even an abstract presentation of this kind must begin by emphasizing once again that the ontological priority of the economy that is stressed by Marx does not involve any kind of hierarchical relationship. It expresses the simple fact that the social existence of the superstructure always ontologically presupposes that of the process of economic reproduction, that all this is ontologically inconceivable without the economy, while it is essential to economic being, on the other hand, that it can not reproduce itself with calling into being a superstructure that corresponds to it, even if in a contradictory way. This rejection of an ontologically based hierarchy is closely linked with the question of how economic value is related to other, social values. With the adjective 'social', we have made a preliminary demarcation, even if at first of a very abstract and declarative character, between our conception of value and the idealist one (in most cases a transcendent one). We believe that the social necessity of the positing of value is with the same ontological necessity both presupposition and result of the alternative character of human social acts. In the choice of alternatives, there is necessarily a decision between the valuable and that which runs contrary to values, and this also contains in it, by ontological necessity, the possibility of a choice of the contra-value as well as of error in a subjective choice of the valuable.

At this stage of our presentation, we can not go into more concrete detail as to the contradictions that arise in this connection, but can merely emphasize a few particularly significant features of the economic alternative. This always involves the transformation of something purely natural into something social, and hence the creation of the material foundations of sociality. In the case of use-value, natural objects are transformed into objects that are suitable and useful for the reproduction of human life. Through the process of its conscious production, the merely natural existence for others receives an essentially new connection to a man who has thus become social, something which could not yet exist in nature. And in so far as in the case of exchange-value, socially necessary labour-time becomes the measure and regulator of the social intercourse of men determined by the economy, the self-constitution of social categories and the retreat of the natural boundary is involved. Value, in the economic sense, is thus the motor for the transformation of the merely natural into the social, the consummation of the humanization of man in his sociality. Because economic categories now function as the vehicle of this transformation, and they alone are in a position to fulfil the function of this transformation, they attain the ontological priority within social being that we have already referred to. This priority has far-reaching consequences for the structure of social categories and their kind of efficacy, particularly that of value. Firstly, economic value is the only value category whose objectivity is crystallized in the form of an immanently effective regularity: this value is at the same time value (alternative project) and objective law. For this reason, its value character is much weakened in the course of history, although such basic value categories as useful and harmful, successful and unsuccessful, etc. directly arise from the economic value alternatives. (It is certainly no accident that the value categories that are directly related to human actions have been long and tenaciously based on or related to the alternative of useful and harmful. It is only at relatively high stages of development of sociality, when its contradictory character has become manifest, that this connection is fundamentally rejected, as with Kant for example). Secondly, as we have already mentioned, the economic category of value works so as to call into being its realization in relations of social mediation that become ever more complicated, in which qualitatively new types of alternatives arise, which cannot be grasped in purely economic terms. It is sufficient to refer to the complex of problems we have already dealt with concerning the increase of human capacities and the integration of the species.

In these realms of mediation, the most varied systems of human values gradually arise. We have already pointed out the socio-ontological fact that is very important in this connection, that each of these mediations stands in a relation to heterogeneity to the economy proper, and fulfils its function of mediation precisely as a result of this heterogeneity, and this must naturally express itself in the heterogenous character of the value arising on this basis—heterogenous in comparison

with economic value. Our earlier discussion also reveals that
this heterogeneity, in certain circumstances, can even develop
to the level of opposition, in so far as two value systems lead
to alternatives which develop from the variation resulting
from heterogeneity to the level of opposition. Situations of
this kind express the fundamental distinction between
economic value and other values: the latter always presuppose
sociality, as an existential characteristic that is already present
and in the process of development, whereas economic value
has not only originally created this sociality, but permanently
produces and reproduces it anew, always on an extended
scale. In this process of reproduction, economic value time
and again receives new patterns, and even quite new forms of
categories can emerge. (We can refer in this connection to
relative surplus-value, which we have repeatedly discussed.)
Yet in this continuous process of change, their basic forms
remain essentially unaltered.[62] Since a non-economic value
form does not produce social being, but rather presupposes
it as for the moment given, and searches out within the
context of the given existence the alternatives and modes of
decision that it has thrown up, the momentary *hic et nunc* of
the social structure and the socially operative tendencies
must be the decisive determinants of its form and content.
Where the economic development produces a genuine alteration in the social structure, a replacement by a qualitatively
different formation, such as the transition from the slave
economy via feudalism to capitalism, there necessarily arise
qualitative changes in the composition and characteristics of
the non-economic value areas. It is not only that spontaneously
self-regulating modes of life are replaced by a conscious
guidance, an institutional control of human behaviour, so that
it is socially necessary for value systems of a completely new
type to emerge; these must also renounce the fixed categorical
pattern that the regular transformation of nature stamps on
economic value. For all their sometimes durable stability, they

seem endowed, in their contents and forms, with a Heraclitean unrest of becoming, and this is necessary, for in order to perform their function, they must develop organically beyond the momentary problematic of the social here and now. Naturally, their characteristics should not be conceived as a unilinear and direct causal dependence, as is the case with vulgar Marxism. This dependence really consists 'simply' in the fact that, at the given stage of social development, certain problems of life are thrown up, that this gives rise to concrete alternatives, and men attempt to find concrete solutions to these. There is thus a dependence in relation to the position, quality and content of the problems and solutions; but since the consequences of economic development, as we have already seen, are very uneven, and since each of them not only represents a social being, but simultaneously and with the same ontological necessity the point of departure for new values, this dependency can be concretized in a non-economic value system radically contradicting the consequences of a stage of economic development and exposing them as anti-values. (We could refer here to the problem of alienation.) This leads to the possible solutions occupying a still broader space within this dependency: their intentions can extend from the immediate actuality through to a direct orientation to the problems of the human race, and their effects can thus stretch from the present to a distant future. Of course this space, however broad, is not unlimited or arbitrary; its point of departure in the concrete here and now of the present stage of economic development ultimately determines in an irrevocable way the social being of the content and form of value.

Given such a deep historical linkage, combined with a variation in realizations too great to survey as a whole, it is easy to understand that their interpretation outside of the Marxian method is likely to lead to a historical relativism. But this is only one aspect of the possible misunderstandings.

For despite their manifold character, the non-economic values in no way constitute an order-less diversity of merely transient particulars. Since their real genesis, however uneven and contradictory, results from an ultimately unified social being in process, and since it is only socially typical and meaningful alternatives that can solidify into genuine values, it would be the antithesis of orderly thought to homogenize them into a purely ideal system governed by logical rules. A systematization of this kind would necessarily ignore their ontological specificity and heterogeneity; not to mention the fact that such a logicization would be a direct de-historicization, in which every value would lose its concrete basis, its real concrete existence, and could only find its place in the system as a formal and faded shadow of itself. Despite this, value systems of this kind, and systematizations of particular values (system of virtues, etc.), have sprung up on a massive scale. But these possess only an ephemeral significance, which is still further reduced by the fact that in most of these cases it is not values themselves, but merely their pallid theoretical reflections, that form the basis of the systematization.

Aristotle's doctrine of value in practical action has had an unusual durability primarily because he never attempted a theoretical systematization, but proceeded in a profound and concrete way, as is extremely seldom done, from the genuine social alternatives of his time, and investigated and discovered the internal dialectical relationships and regularities of their realization. But even the much poorer and more abstract 'categorical imperative' owes its often renewed popularity to its relative abstention from logical systematics; where Kant attempts to determine concrete possibilities of action, at least in a negative and prohibiting way, by means of logical deductions, the questionable character of his position becomes evident. (We could refer to the negative criticisms of Hegel and Simmel, oriented in opposing directions.) The doctrine of value thus acquires a false antinomy in the history of thought: historical relativism on the one hand, logical and systematizing dogmatism on the other. It is no accident that, particularly in periods of crisis and transition, thinkers with a pronounced sense for concrete reality in the problem of values have consciously chosen an anti-systematic and frequently a purely aphoristic mode of expression (La Rochefoucauld).

The ontological *tertium datur* to this antinomy is based on the real continuity of the socio-historical process. In this connection, we must come back to the new conception of substantiality that we put forward, which is not counterposed in a rigid and exclusive way to the process of becoming, as a static and stationary relationship of conservation, but rather as something in process, changing itself in process, renewing itself, taking part in the process, and yet preserving itself in essence. The genuine values that arise in the process of sociality can only be maintained and preserved in this way. We must of course radically reject here an 'eternal' validity of values beyond the process. These values arose without exception at a definite stage in the course of the social process, and indeed as real values, not in such a way that the process merely effected a realization of an intrinsically 'eternal' value; values themselves have a real birth in the social process, and in part also a real death. The continuity of substance in social being is the continuity of man, his growth, his problematic, his alternatives. And so far as a value, in its reality and its concrete realizations, is involved in this process, becomes an effective component of it, and embodies an essential element of its social existence, it thus acquires the substantiality of value itself, its nature and its reality. This is clearly displayed in the constancy of genuine values, which is certainly not absolute, but rather social and historical. The two sides of the antinomy of relativism and dogmatism, which was formerly insurpassable, are supported by the fact that the historical process permanently reproduces both change and constancy in change. The constancy of certain ethical positions as well as of possibilities of objectification in the area of art is just as striking as is the process of rise and fall. For this reason, only the new conception of substantiality that we have emphasized, and that is objectified here too as continuity, can form the methodological basis for the solution of this antinomy.

The fact that this process, like every process in society, is an uneven one, and that the continuity is expressed at times in the form of a long disappearance, and now and then as a sudden actualization, in no way alters this connection between continuity and substance in social being, or the efficacy of continuity in its reproduction. In connection with uneven development, we have touched on Marx's views on Homer. Marx raises there this problem of continuity of aesthetic being. He does not see the really decisive problem in the genesis of value from social development; he rather formulates the value problem as follows: 'But the difficulty lies not in understanding that the Greek arts and epic are bound up with certain forms of social development. The difficulty is that they still afford us artistic pleasure and that in a certain respect they count as a norm and as an unattainable model.'[63] The solution that Marx indicates is based on continuity in the development of the human species. And when Lenin speaks of the possibilities of the second phase of socialism, i.e. of communism, in his *State and Revolution*, he focusses his attention on men becoming 'accustomed' to conditions of life that are worthy of humanity. The content of this, according to Lenin, consists in the fact that, 'freed from capitalist slavery, from the untold horrors, savagery, absurdities and infamies of capitalist exploitation, people will gradually *become accustomed* to observing the elementary rules of social intercourse that have been known for centuries and repeated for thousands of years in all copy-book maxims.

They will become accustomed to observing them without force, without coercion, without subordination, *without the special apparatus* for coercion called the state.'[64] Lenin thus refers to the same continuity of human development as does Marx. This concrete and real substantiality of the process in its continuity abolishes the false dilemma between relativism and dogmatism. It is perhaps not superfluous to give this construction of the social continuity of values a more concrete form by establishing the fact that its actual direction points from the past to the future; regressions to the past always involve an orientation to present practice, i.e. to the future. The one-sided interpretation that is frequently met with, which relates the present to its 'sources' in the past, can thus very easily falsify the real circumstances.

This sketch of Marx's ontology is necessarily extremely incomplete, and very far even from adequately dealing with just the main problems of its significance; in the second part, we shall make the supplementary attempt to make up for these omissions, at least with respect to some central problems. But the present discussion can not be concluded without at least a few more detailed indications as to the relation of the perspective of socialist development to Marx's general ontological conception. It is well-known that Marx demarcated his conception of socialism first and foremost as scientific, as against the utopian conception. If we examine this distinction from the standpoint of Marx's ontology, the first decisive aspect that strikes us is that Marx sees socialism as the normal and necessary product of the internal dialectic of social being, of the self-development of the economy with all its presuppositions and consequences, as well as of the class struggle, whereas for the utopians, a development that was in many respects essentially defective had to be corrected by decisions, experiments, provision of models, etc. This means in particular that the ontologically central role of the economy not only makes possible the rise of socialism, but that its ontological importance and function cannot cease even under an achieved socialism. In *Capital,* Marx speaks of how the economic sphere must always remain, even under socialism, a 'realm of necessity' in human life. Marx thus counters Fourier, whose genial critical insights he valued highly, but who believed that under socialism labour would change into a form of play; he also rejects, if without any definite polemic, all those ideas according to which socialism would introduce an era 'without economics'. In the objective ontological sense, the path to socialism is that of the development we have already described, in which through labour, through the economic world it has created, and through the immanent dialectic of this as its motor, social being develops to its proper nature, the specificity of the human race as something conscious, not simply natural and dumb. The economy leads to an ever higher sociality of social categories. But this is only achieved in class societies in the form that it is objectified to men as a 'second nature'. This basic characteristic of an objectivity completely independent of individual alternative acts remains insurpassable; Marx expresses this with the term 'realm of necessity'. The qualitative leap consists in the domination of this 'second nature' as well by humanity, something that cannot be achieved by any class society. Contemporary capitalism, for example, must make the whole sphere of consumption into a 'second nature' that dominates man in an unprecedented way.

The peculiarity of capitalism is that it produces a social production spontaneously, in the true sense of this term; socialism transforms this spontaneity into conscious regulation. In the introductory and basic statements in which he explains the economy as the 'realm of necessity', Marx says of the economy of socialism: 'Freedom in this field can only consist in socialized man, the associated producers, rationally regulating their interchange with Nature, bringing it under their common control, instead of being ruled by it as by the blind forces of Nature; and achieving this with the least expenditure of energy and under conditions most favourable to, and worthy of, their human nature.' It is only on this basis that the realm of freedom can emerge. 'Beyond it begins that development of human energy which is an end in itself, the true realm of freedom, which, however, can blossom forth only with this realm of necessity as its basis.'[65] At this point Marx's ontology, which is so often misunderstood by his followers, becomes clearly visible. With an unbeatable rigour, he establishes that the economy alone, the process whereby social being becomes social, can produce this phase of human development; that this is not only the way for this ultimate self-attainment of man, but also the indispensable and permanent ontological basis for it, and must remain so. Every theoretical tendency that seeks other preconditions for socialism inevitably falls back into utopianism. At the same time, it becomes apparent, as we have already repeatedly pointed out, that the economy is only the basis, only what is ontologically primary, and that it gives rise to the human capacities and the forces of social complexes that actually produce the realization of what is economically necessary, which accelerate, reinforce, promote its development as social reality, and in certain circumstances can also inhibit or divert it.

This dialectical contradiction between, on the one hand, the economically necessary development of social being and, on the other, the concrete contradictions between the social prerequisites and results of economic formations and the extra-economic social factors (such as force, etc.) has also been an important basis of uneven development in earlier history. The concrete alternatives as forms of any human behaviour return at every historical turning-point at a higher level. It is a matter of course that Marx, since he maintained the ontological priority of the economic even under socialism, also refers to the alternative involved in its genesis. In the *Communist Manifesto*, already, he writes with respect to the class struggle and the rise of new and more highly structured economic formations: 'Freeman and slave, patrician and plebeian, lord and serf, guild-master and journeyman, in a word, oppressor and oppressed, stood in constant opposition to one another, carried on an uninterrupted, now hidden, now open fight, a fight that each time ended, either in a revolutionary reconstitution of society at large, or in the common ruin of the contending classes.'[66] This alternative character which marks the historical development as a whole, does not abolish the ontological priority and ultimately decisive role of the economy, but gives it a concrete socio-historical concreteness, has been very much reduced by Marx's successors, and has often even completely vanished. It has partly been simplified into a vulgar materialist mechanical 'necessity', and partly led the neo-Kantian or positivist opposition to this vulgarization into a historical agnosticism. Lenin alone held firmly to the original Marxist conception and considered it the guiding principle of revolutionary practice, particularly in difficult and complicated situations. It was so in the decision on the insurrection that aimed at the proletarian seizure of power on 7th November 1917. Lenin expressed the theoretical foundation of positions of this kind completely in the sense of the Marxian conception, as in 1920 at the Second Congress of the Communist International, when he conducted a two-sided polemic, both against those who trivialized the great crisis of that time, and against those who saw there being no way out for the bourgeoisie. In Lenin's words, 'There is no such thing as an absolutely hopeless situation.' To try to 'prove' this theoretically 'would be sheer pedantry, or playing with concepts and catchwords. Practice alone can serve as real "proof" in this and similar questions.'[67] This practice is of an alternative character.

Lenin thus presents the path to socialism in complete

162

accordance with the general socio-historical ontology of Marx. This also takes the form of opposition to all conceptions that assume as 'end to history'; in Marx's time this was first and foremost a question of the utopians, who considered socialism as an ultimate condition worthy of humanity that was to be brought into being once and for all. For Marx, there was even here the question of the further progress of history. In his Preface to *A Contribution...*, Marx writes of socialism: 'This social formation brings, therefore, the prehistory of human society to a close.'[68] The term 'pre-history' is chosen with care and has a double significance here. On the one hand, the implicit but still decisive rejection of any form of the end of history. The expression used by Marx was however also designed, on the other hand, to directly demarcate the particular character of the new section of history. We have repeatedly emphasized that new ontological stages of a social being are not just suddenly there, but—just as in the organic realm—gradually develop into their proper, immanent and purest form in the course of a historical process. In the remarks leading up to the conclusion just quoted, Marx indicates the antagonism in capitalist society as the decisive difference between this and socialism. In general, this feature is presented from the socialist side in such a way that the end of class society simultaneously abolishes its necessarily antagonistic character. This is correct in very general terms, but it still requires a not unimportant addition in relation to the problem that we discussed earlier, the relation between economic value and the objective values of social life as a whole.

Since values are always realized by way of behaviour, actions, etc., it is clear that their existence cannot be separated from the alternatives involved in their realization. The opposition between what is valuable and what is contrary to value is thus insuperably present in the decision contained in any teleological project. It is quite different with the contents and forms of value themselves. In certain societies, these can stand in an antagonistic relation to the economic process, and they do so at the most varied stages of economic development, in capitalism too in a very significant form. The abolition of the antinomy referred to by Marx is thus related to this complex of problems as well: and correspondingly to the basic ontological structure of social being, which is again in the closest connection with the properties of the economic sphere. In the statements just quoted, where Marx talks of the realms of necessity and freedom, what is referred to is not just an economically optimal rationality in the arrangement of economic development, but also the fact that this arrangement is achieved 'under conditions most favourable to, and worthy of, their human nature'. Here we have the economic basis for the abolition of the antinomy between economic and extra-economic values clearly expressed, again in full agreement with the basic conception that Marx always put forward. Already in the *Economic and Philosophical Manuscripts* Marx considered the relationship between man and wife as the 'natural species-relation'. This is correct and important in a dual sense. On the one hand, the basis of human life is realized in this relationship in an insurpassable immediacy, while on the other hand it is realized in the course of human development in the forms that are impressed on it by production in the broadest sense.* It follows that there is a permanent and permanently reproduced antagonism between economic necessity and its results for the development of the human species. The fact that this antagonism only very gradually appears in conscious form, that its emergence for a long while (up till today) only slowly outstrips its sporadic beginnings and is frequently objectified as false consciousness, once more shows the general historical character of such developments, but does not change anything essential in the ontological foundations of the connection between values. This is why Marx could say of the sexual relation, this time in

164

agreement with Fourier, 'From this relationship one can therefore judge man's whole level of development.'[69] Here,
precisely in the robust everyday character of this situation,
the value antagonism, this time between economic progress
and 'man's whole level of development', is clearly visible.[70]

Recognition of the insurpassable efficacy of alternatives, in
every case where the social and practical synthesis of human
actions is involved, does not contradict, as we have seen, the
regularity of the main tendency in economic development.
Thus Marx could precisely define in theoretical terms the
general necessity of the cyclical character of the capitalist
economy of his time, and therefore also the necessity of
crises. This too was simply a general recognition of tendencies
and perspectives, which never led Marx to claim that it was
possible thereby to predict the time and place of the outbreak
of individual crises, even approximately. Marx's prospective
predictions for socialism should also be considered from this
methodological standpoint. It is particularly in the *Critique
of the Gotha Programme* that Marx investigates these most
general economic tendencies, particularly thoroughly in the
case of the first transitional phase. He establishes here that the
structure of commodity exchange, despite all otherwise
fundamental changes, will function in this phase in the same
way as in capitalism: 'Here obviously the same principle
prevails as that which regulates the exchange of commodities,
as far as this is exchange of equal values. Content and form
are changed, because under the altered circumstances no one
can give anything except his labour, and because, on the
other hand, nothing can pass to the ownership of individuals
except individual means of consumption. But, as far as the
distribution of the latter among the individual producers is
concerned, the same principle prevails as in the exchange of
commodity-equivalents: a given amount of labour in one form
is exchanged for an equal amount of labour in another form.'
This has very far-reaching consequences for the socially

decisive systems of mediation. For all the transformations of the class structure that socialism brings about, right remains essentially an equal right and is consequently 'bourgeois right', although in many ways its former antinomic character is abolished or at least weakened. Marx goes on to show: 'This *equal* right is an unequal right for unequal labour. It recognises no class differences, because everyone is only a worker like everyone else; but it tacitly recognizes unequal individual endowment and thus productive capacity as natural privileges. *It is, therefore, a right of inequality, in its content, like every other right.*' It is only at a higher phase, the economic preconditions of which Marx indicates, as well as the human preconditions made socially possible by the economy, that the situation 'From each according to his ability, to each according to his needs'[71] becomes objectively possible. The structure of commodity exchange, the effectiveness of the law of value for individual men as consumers, now ceases. It is evident of course that in production itself, socially necessary labour-time and hence the law of value as regulator of production must remain unchanged in their validity even with the growth of the productive forces.

These are generally necessary tendencies of development, and can therefore be scientifically established in this generality. The first part has already proved its validity; verification of the further prospect can only be provided by the facts of the future. It would however be senseless to believe that we could obtain from what are deliberately extremely general perspectives, direct conclusions for concrete tactical or even strategic decisions, a direct signpost. Lenin was precisely aware of this. When the question arose of introducing state capitalism in the context of the New Economic Policy, he said that there was no book of guidelines for this problem. 'It did not occur even to Marx to write a word on this subject, and he died without leaving a single precise statement or definite instruction on it.'[72] Here too, it was only with Stalin that the bad habit arose of 'deducing' every strategic or tactical decision as a direct and logically necessary consequence of the teachings of Marx and Lenin, which led to principles being mechanically adapted to the needs of the day, and thus distorted, so that the distinction between general laws and unique concrete decisions, which is so important, simply vanished, to give way to a voluntarist and practicist dogmatism. These indications already show how important it is, from the standpoint of practice also, to re-establish the ontology that Marx put forward in his works. So far we have naturally concentrated on the theoretical results that follow from this. But we shall only grasp these in their full significance when we survey the ambit of their efficacy in the second part, applying them to individual key problems, in a more concrete and precise fashion than has been possible in these general discussions.

NOTES

Section 1
*   (p. 1) Cf. Lukács, *Hegel's False and his Genuine Ontology*, Part One, Chapter III of 'The Ontology of Social Being'.
1   Engels, 'Ludwig Feuerbach', Marx and Engels *Selected Works* [one volume edition], London, 1970, p. 596.
2   Lenin, *Philosophical Notebooks* (vol. 38 of Lenin's *Collected Works*), pp. 169, 190, 234.
3   *Collected Works,* vol. 5, p. 41.
4   *Collected Works,* vol. 1, p. 104.
5   'The German Ideology', *Collected Works,* vol. 5, p. 28.
6.   *Capital,* Vol. I, Moscow, 1961, pp. 42-43.
7   ibid., pp. 177, 179, 178.
*   (p. 6) Cf. Lukács, *Labour,* Part Two, Chapter I of 'The Ontology of Social Being'.
8   *Grundrisse,* Harmondsworth, 1973, p. 105.
9   *Capital,* Vol. I, p. 38.
10   ibid., p. 83.
11   Marx to Engels, 19 December, 1860; *Marx-Engels-Werke,* Berlin, 1957-64, vol. 30, p. 131.
12   In particular, important passages in Marx's first criticism of Hegel: 'Critique of Hegel's Doctrine of the State' in *Early Writings,* Harmondsworth, 1975, pp. 154ff.
13   *Capital,* Vol. I, pp. 103-104.
14   Engels, *Dialectics of Nature,* Moscow, 1972, p. 25.
15   Hobbes, *Leviathan,* part one, chapter XI.
16   *Capital,* Vol. III, Moscow, 1962, p. 797.
17   Cf. *Dialectics of Nature,* p. 50.
18   I must thank Agnes Heller for drawing my attention to this aspect of Machiavelli's theory.
19   Lenin, *Philosophical Notebooks,* p. 180.
20   ibid., p. 359.
21   ibid., p. 319.
22   There were a whole series of attempts of this kind, from Gramsci to Caudwell. My own book *History and Class Consciousness* also arose out of these aspirations. However the reductionist and schematizing pressure of Stalin soon put a stop to such tendencies in the Communist International— the only place where they could take root. These attempts differed greatly in maturity and correctness, and they need to be investigated without prejudice or tendentious over- or under-valuation. Research of this kind is so far confined to that in Italy on Gramsci.

Section 2

1   'Economic and Philosophical Manuscripts of 1844' in *Early Writings,*
    loc. cit., p. 390.
2   'The Poverty of Philosophy', *Collected Works,* vol. 6, pp. 166-7.
3   'The Holy Family', *Collected Works,* vol. 4, pp. 120ff.
4   'The German Ideology', *Collected Works,* vol. 5, p. 78.
5   'Speech at the Graveside of Karl Marx', *Selected Works* [three-volume
    edition], vol. 3, p. 162.
6   *Selected Works,* [one-volume edition], p. 181.
7   ibid.,
8   *Capital,* Vol. I, p. 167.
9   ibid., p. 171.
10 ibid., pp. 234-5.
11 ibid., p. 760.
*   (p. 36) In the manuscript, this is followed by the note: 'Of course, it is
    still not possible to know today how much is eventually to be found in the
    original manuscripts. Riazanov told me in the early 1930s that the manu-
    scripts of *Capital* would make ten volumes altogether, and that what
    Engels published was only a part of this mass of manuscripts.'
*   (p. 40) Cf. Lukács, *Hegel's False and his Genuine Ontology,* loc. cit.
12 *Capital,* Vol. I, p. 61.
13 loc. cit., pp. 375 ff.
14 *Capital,* Vol. I, p. 74.
15 ibid., p. 51 n.
16 *Theories of Surplus-Value,* Part II, Moscow, 1968, pp. 117-8; see also,
    for more detail, *Grundrisse,* pp. 408 ff.
17 *Capital,* Vol. II, Moscow 1961, p. 394.
18 ibid., p. 100.
19 ibid., p. 395.
20 I must thank Franz Janossy for drawing my attention to this problem.
21 *Grundrisse,* p. 90.
22 ibid., p. 94.
23 ibid., pp. 91-92. It would be instructive for those who seek at any cost to
    construct an opposition between the young and the mature Marx, to
    compare this passage with that on the development of music and musicality
    in the *Economic and Philosophical Manuscripts.* Here, where Marx
    considers the *'cultivation* of the five senses' as a product of the entire
    former history of the world, he formulates the same idea in a similarly
    universal way. (loc. cit., p. 353).
24 *Grundrisse,* p. 92.
25 ibid., p. 94.
26 ibid., p. 96.
27 ibid., p. 98.
28 Lenin, *Collected Works,* vol. 13, pp. 238 ff.
29 *Capital,* Vol. III, p. 771.

Section 3

1   It is evident that a category like leisure, which is so decisive for the whole of human culture, is most closely connected with this developmental tendency. We shall only be able to deal with it in the second part.

2   Marx, 'The Eighteenth Brumaire of Louis Bonaparte', *Selected Works* [one-volume edition], p. 96.

3   *The Holy Family*, Moscow, 1956, pp. 162 ff.

4   *The German Ideology*, Moscow, 1964, p. 93.

5   *Grundrisse*, pp. 487-8.

6   ibid.

7   ibid.

8   *The Poverty of Philosophy*, New York, 1963, pp. 11, 12.

9   *The Origin of the Family, Private Property and the State*, London, 1972, p. 161.

10   *Capital*, Vol. I, pp. 42-3.

11   ibid., pp. 76 ff.

12   *Grundrisse*, p. 109.

13   See Engels to Schmidt, 27 October 1890; *Selected Correspondence*, Moscow, 1965, pp. 419 ff.

14   See Marx, 'A Review of Guizot's Book "Why has the English Revolution been Successful?" ', *Articles on Britain*, Moscow, 1971, pp. 89 ff.

*   (p. 101) Cf. Lukács, *Labour* (Part Two, Chapter I of 'The Ontology of Social Being.'

15   ' "Left-Wing" Communism, An Infantile Disorder', *Collected Works*, vol. 31, p. 95.

16   *Theories of Surplus-Value*, Part II, Moscow, 1968, pp. 508 and 509.

17   *Grundrisse*, p. 110.

18   Quoted, with agreement, by Lenin; *Philosophical Notebooks*, p. 135.

19   *Selected Correspondence*, p. 313.

20   *Selected Works*, pp. 96 ff.

21   *Grundrisse*, p. 102.

22   ibid.

23   ibid., p. 103.

24   ibid., p. 105.

25   *Capital*, Vol. I, p. 8.

26   *The Origin of the Family. . .*, pp. 228 and 181.

27   *Capital*, Vol. I, p. 737.

28   ibid., p. 10.

29   *Collected Works*, vol. 31, pp. 21 and 64.

30   *Grundrisse*, p. 109.

31   loc. cit., p. 85.

32   The point we have just discussed emerges repeatedly in Marx's early writings with particular reference to Germany. Cf. for example, 'Critique of Hegel's Doctrine of the State,' *Early Writings*, p. 252.

33   It is self-evident that all these factors of unevenness can only be rationally

understood *post festum*, but this in no way abolishes the unevenness. The surprisingly rapid reception of capitalism in Japan, in comparison to other backward countries, is thus not difficult to explain in terms of its feudal structure, in contrast to the Asiatic relations of production as in China and India. This case was however necessary, in order for knowledge to comprehend, from the standpoint of economic rationality, the particularly favourable character of the dissolving feudal society for the transition to capitalism.

34 The geographical situation is obviously also a natural basis, but in the course of historical development it acquires an overwhelmingly social determination. Whether the sea separates or unites two countries is essentially determined by the level of development of the productive forces. The higher this is, the more the natural boundary retreats, in this case also.

35 Lenin, 'Imperialism, the Highest Stage of Capitalism', *Collected Works*, vol. 22, pp. 273 ff.

36 *Grundrisse*, p. 109.

37 Marx to Lassalle, 22 July, 1861, *Marx-Engels-Werke*, vol. 30, p. 614. Engels' letter to Conrad Schmidt, referred to below, is printed in *Selected Correspondence*, pp. 419 ff.

38 *MEW* 30, pp. 614 ff.

39 H. Kelsen, *Hauptprobleme der Staatsrechtslehre*, 1911, p. 411. Kant expresses in a less paradoxical form this incongruency, which naturally presents itself most clearly in extreme cases such as revolutions, saying that the revolution certainly denies any existing legality, but that the laws of the victorious revolution can and must claim full legal validity; Kant, *Metaphysik der Sitten*, Leipzig, 1907, pp. 44 ff. It is beside the point here that this modern conception of law was preceded by a long period of the so-called right of resistance, whose echoes can still be found in Fichte and even in Lassalle. The social duality and heterogeneity between the genesis and the validity of law thereby undergoes only a change in appearance, not in the ontological essence, the less so in that this contradiction in the right of resistance itself also involves a juridical mode of appearance, even if in forms different from those in modern law.

40 Engels refers, in the letter quoted earlier [note 37], to the presence of this possibility in any political decision in relation to the economy, and correctly points out that major errors in decision can lead to great harm, even though this does not decisively alter the main line of economic development.

41 *Grundrisse*, p. 110.

42 Cf. *Theories of Surplus-Value*, Part I, pp. 275 ff.

43 *Grundrisse*, p. 110.

44 G. Lukács, Werke Band 12, *Die Eigenart des Ästhetischen*, Neuwied/ Rhein, 1963, II, 375 ff. and 448 ff.

45 'Eighteenth Brumaire. . .', *Selected Works* [one volume edition], pp. 96 ff.

46   'The Holy Family', *Collected Works*, vol. 4, p. 170.
47   Engels to Margaret Harkness, April 1888, *Selected Correspondence*, pp. 402-3.
48   'The German Ideology', *Collected Works*, vol. 5, p. 4.
49   ibid., p. 44.
50   loc. cit., p. 373.
51   ibid., p. 329
52   ibid., p. 350.
53   Conversation with Soret, 5 January 1832, *Goethes Gespräche mit Eckermann*, Insel-Ausgabe, Leipzig, n.d., p. 702.
54   *Grundrisse*, p. 84.
55   'The Holy Family', *Collected Works*, vol. 4, pp. 120-1.
56   *Capital*, Vol. I, p. 358.
57   *Grundrisse*, p. 109.
58   Max Weber, *Gesammelte Aufsätze zur Wissenschaftslehre*, Tübingen, 1922, pp. 545 ff.
59   G. Plekhanov, *Fundamental Problems of Marxism*, London 1969, p. 80.
60   *Selected Works* [one-volume edition], p. 181.
61   Engels to Bloch, 21 September 1890, *Selected Correspondence*, p. 417. See also the letter to Mehring of 14 July 1893, loc. cit., p. 458.
62   Marx shows in *Capital* how socially necessary labour-time remains essentially unchanged in the most varied formations; Vol. I, pp. 76 ff.
63   *Grundrisse*, p. 110.
64   Lenin, *Collected Works*, vol. 25, p. 462.
65   *Capital*, Vol. III, p. 800.
66   *Selected Works* [one-volume edition], pp. 35-6.
67   *Collected Works*, vol. 31, p. 227.
68   *Selected Works* [one-volume edition], p. 182.
*   (p. 164) This is followed in the manuscript by the note: 'Recent ethnographical research shows how this relationship is already determined at primitive stages of economic development, as a result of the social structure.'
69   'Economic and Philosophical Manuscripts', loc. cit., p. 347.
70   Here we are concerned exclusively with Marx's views. As I have frequently asserted, the realization of socialism under Stalin proceeded by other paths, which were at times completely contrary. We must simply insist here, in order not to allow any misunderstandings of method, on our opposition to all those theories that identify the Stalinist development of socialism with Marx's conception, by presenting the theory and practice of Stalin as in agreement with Marx and Lenin, whether this is in order to cover the erroneous decisions made with false appeals to Marx, and thus to perpetuate them, or alternatively in order to compromise socialism in general. Without being able to go into any more detail here on this major complex of problems, it must just be said that it is extremely naive (or else demagogical) to see the question of a fundamentally new social formation

as finally settled after what is, considered historically, so short a period. Even if decades are still necessary in order to overcome the Stalinist legacy, in theory and in practice, and to return to Marxism, such a space of time is still relatively short from the historical standpoint.

71   'Critique of the Gotha Programme', *Selected Works* [one-volume edition], pp. 319 ff.

72   *Collected Works,* vol. 33, p. 278.

Georg Lukács: TOWARD THE ONTOLOGY OF SOCIAL
BEING

Part Two: THE MOST IMPORTANT PROBLEMS
I. *Labour*
    1.   Labour as a Teleological Project
    2.   Labour as a Model of Social Practice
    3.   The Subject-Object Relation in Labour and its Consequences

II. *Reproduction*
    1.   General Problems of Reproduction
    2.   Complexes of Complexes
    3.   Problems of Ontological Priority
    4.   The Reproduction of Man in Society
    5.   The Reproduction of Society as a Totality

III. *The Realm of Ideas and Ideology*
    1.   The Role of the Ideal in the Economy
    2.   Toward an Ontology of the Ideal Moment
    3.   The Problem of Ideology

VI. *Alienation*
    1.   The General Ontological Features of Alienation
    2.   The Ideological Aspects of Alienation; Religion as Alienation
    3.   The Objective Foundation of Alienation and its Abolition; The Contemporary Form of Alienation

CPSIA information can be obtained
at www.ICGtesting.com
Printed in the USA
BVHW042348230222
629915BV00006B/734